THE
GREAT WAR ILLUSTRATED
CALL TO ARMS
OVER BY CHRISTMAS

THE
GREAT WAR ILLUSTRATED
CALL TO ARMS
OVER BY CHRISTMAS

Outbreak of War

David Bilton

Pen & Sword
MILITARY

First published in Great Britain in 2016 by
PEN & SWORD MILITARY
an imprint of
Pen & Sword Books Ltd,
47 Church Street, Barnsley,
South Yorkshire.
S70 2AS

ISBN 978 1 47383 3 722

A CIP catalogue record for this book is available
from the British Library

Printed and bound in England by CPI Group (UK) Ltd, Croydon, CR0 4YY

Pen & Sword Books Ltd incorporates the imprints of
Pen & Sword Aviation, Pen & Sword Maritime,
Pen & Sword Military, Pen & Sword Select, Pen & Sword Military Classics,
Leo Cooper, Wharncliffe Local History

For a complete list of Pen & Sword titles please contact:
PEN & SWORD BOOKS LIMITED
47 Church Street, Barnsley, South Yorkshire, S70 2AS, England.
E-mail: enquiries@pen-and-sword.co.uk
Website: www.pen-and-sword.co.uk

Contents

Acknowledgements 6

Introduction 7

The Home Front 9

Section 1   *The pre-war world* 15

Section 2   *Mobilisation, recruiting and departure* 23

Section 3   *Getting ready for war* 61

Section 4   *Wartime life* 83

Section 5   *Propaganda* 99

Section 6   *Casualties* 111

Section 7   *Personalities* 129

Section 8   *Refugees* 141

Section 9   *News* 151

Section 10   *Raids and occupation* 157

Section 11   *Joining in* 169

Section 12   *Christmas* 179

Day by day chronology 183

Bibliography 187

Index 189

Acknowledgements

As with previous books, a great big thank you to Anne Coulson for her help in checking the text and to the staff of The Prince Consort's Library and Reading Central Library for their help, kindness and knowledge during the pre-writing stages of this book.

Errors of omission or commission are mine alone.

Introduction

This book is the first volume in a series that will show life on the Home Front during each year of the war. It is profusely illustrated with photographs, artwork, ephemera, illustrations, cartoons, newspaper clippings and advertisements to show how life was seen through the eyes of those not in the military frontline. It is not just about one country; and although the major part of it records life in Britain, I have attempted to show the international commonality of various themes by using illustrations wherever possible from across the world. Though readers will be familiar with some, most have not been published since the war, while many have never been published.

This a book about the Home Front on an international scale. It is not chronological and, although themed, topics do cross over between themes. Similarly, the difference between being in the forces and being on the Home Front can seem a grey area. However, it took a long time to train new recruits, and that training was done on the Home Front. In many areas there were more people in uniform than out of it; a fact that became accepted as part of life.

What was 'The Home Front?' There are many interpretations of the phrase: 'the sphere of civilian activity in war'; 'the civilian sector of a nation at war when its armed forces are in combat abroad'; 'the name given to the part of war that was not actively involved in the fighting but which was vital to it'; an 'informal term for the civilian populace of the nation at war as an active support system of their military. Military forces depend on "home front" civilian support services such as factories that build material to support the military front'; it 'refers to life in Britain during the war itself'. All of these have elements of truth but none fully describe the range of experiences that shaped the Home Front.

If this book is about life away from the combat zone, then some of what happened on the Home Front cannot be recorded here. For those caught in a Zeppelin raid, the Home Front became a war zone; it was not always 'All quiet on the Home Front' as assumed by the title of one oral history book. In this and following volumes, I define the Home Front as the totality of the experience of the civilian population in a country affected, directly or indirectly, by the war. As there were considerable numbers of military personnel on the Home Front, who interacted with the civilian population, they too are included.

This again needs some examination. The Home Front was not a singular experience. Life in the countryside was different to that in the town or city, the latter being more quickly affected by change. However, life in the backwaters of the Scottish Isles was different from life in the Kent countryside. Again, life in a coastal town on the east of the country was unlike that on the west. Of course the whole country experienced a basic similarity but there were many factors that varied the war's effects. How could a family who lost their only son experience the same war as a neighbour with five serving sons who all returned? What similarities were there between the family of a conscientious objector and one whose father/husband had been killed? Or between an Irish family and a Welsh one?

While there is a common link between all of these examples, what is the link between a Belgian, French, Dutch, German, Japanese or Russian family? All these countries had a Home Front and all were directly affected by the war. There are some obvious differences. Neutral Holland was quickly affected by the war on its borders, and Japan, an isolated Allied Power, fought in the Pacific and escorted convoys to Europe. Both were unlike the other countries which, despite some differences, were all united by an invasion, long or short, of their Home Fronts.

We can now add further layers to the civilian experience of the war through the Home Front. Neutral countries had to defend themselves against possible aggression and were on a war footing which inevitably affected civilian life. They were not at war, so nationals of the warring countries were free to move about as before the war and spying was rife. As safe havens, they became the guardians of hundreds of refugees or prisoners of war. And, as in the warring countries, commodities became short because, once at sea, their ships became targets.

Combatant countries on the continent experienced two types of Home Front, the obvious one being the civilians behind the fighting front. But in an occupied country civilians were behind both sides of the line. All shared the same nationality, but lived on the Home Front, very differently, enduring different constraints.

This book therefore illustrates life on the Home Front for civilians on both sides of the wire.

The Home Front

'July 1914: in Britain, France and Germany it was a time of holiday. The "season" was ending and fashionable folk were leaving town for spas, country estates and smart resorts.' While 'in the cities, working men looked forward to an annual day trip to the coast, and imagined the boisterous variety shows they would enjoy with wives and girlfriends. Children in quiet schoolrooms and deafening mills alike fidgeted with excitement at the thought of Punch and Judy tents and ice-cream carts on the promenade.'

On the surface little appeared to be different to last year; Europe was at peace and had been for some considerable time. 'It was as if this was just one more summer in Europe's long span of unbroken peace. But appearance belied the reality.'

The question of whether the war was inevitable or not, and the background to the war, are beyond the remit of this book, but by the end of the month Serbia and the Austro-Hungarian Empire were at war. Although this was noted by many in Britain, it was not a major cause for widespread concern and people continued to plan for the coming Bank Holiday. They were not worried about going to war. As the '*John Bull*' posters on the buses said, 'TO HELL WITH SERBIA!' and 'not a British life shall be sacrificed for the sake of a Russian Hegemony of the Slav world', the liberal *Daily News* told its readers. Anyway Britain had the Irish problem to think about. It was to be business as usual, a motto that would continue well into the war.

It was different in Germany. Mounting tension there found relief on the night of 25 July when Austria's ultimatum to Serbia expired. 'Huge throngs paraded Berlin's Unter den Linden and demonstrated outside the Reichstag and Austrian Embassy. Serbian flags were burned and Serbian residents attacked.' On his return from a Norwegian cruise two days later, the Kaiser was 'greeted by cheering thousands.' The night-time air echoed with 'Deutschland, Deutschland über Alles.'

Fear of the future took hold. 'Silver and small change began to disappear, and bank depositors made large withdrawals of gold. Customers queued to remove their savings from the municipal banks, Stock Exchange values slumped disastrously and, by the 29th, when paper money was refused in the provinces, people were crowding to Berlin in search of gold. That evening several private banks suspended payment. Meanwhile food prices rose steeply as anxious citizens rushed to buy provisions.'

In France, President Poincaré and Premier Viviani, returning unexpectedly from their State visit to Russia drove through cheering crowds. 'As in Germany, there was a sudden run on the banks and a shortage of gold and small currency; and as a precaution the Paris Bourse closed.'

Britain was slower to react. It was only on 31 July, when the bank rate was raised to 8%, possible currency regulations were announced, and the Stock Exchange closed, that the public realised war might be imminent. That same day the Kaiser decreed a 'state of danger of war'. The military took over. 'All banks and public buildings were guarded by sentries with fixed bayonets, and armed police moved in to close food shops that were contravening the price-regulation orders and to enforce the acceptance of paper money.' Early in the evening the Kaiser gave a short ominous speech from his palace balcony. 'This is a dark day and a dark hour…the sword is being forced into my hand…this war will demand of us enormous sacrifice in life and money, but we shall show our foes what it is to provoke Germany.'

That same day both France and Russia had received Germany's ultimatum. The next day the French proclaimed a 'state of siege' throughout France and Algeria and thousands of mobilisation orders were put up 'on the walls of town halls, post offices and schools throughout the country' at the same time as Germany's order. The French mobilisation was to take place after midnight but by evening many men were making their way to their home depot. There was no spontaneous mass outpouring in France in contrast to the experience of Berliners who had flocked to the palace while the cathedral bells tolled for war service. When mobilisation was announced, the crowds broke into the hymn 'Now thank we all our God'. News spread rapidly down the Unter den Linden and 'special news-sheets were rushed on to the streets bearing the proclamation: "The Emperor has ordered a general mobilisation of all the armed forces of the Empire".' No doubt the irony of signing the order on a desk made of wood from Nelson's flagship, HMS *Victory,* a present from Queen Victoria, escaped those present.

The next day both countries mobilised with trained able-bodied men flocking to the colours. Enthusiasm in France was muted and was generally only displayed at 'the leave-takings with the troops', marching columns being pelted with flowers. So many men were on the move that in Berlin, after an open-air service in the Konigsplatz, the 30,000 civilians and reservists who had attended had to walk because all forms of public transport were full.

All of this dampened the holiday spirit in Britain where the deteriorating situation triggered a similar response as in France and Germany. With news that food prices had risen by 75% in Germany, many rushed to buy what they could. 'People were seen loading cars and taxis with provisions, and one London firm reported eight days' business done in one day.' Naturally prices rose and some shops rationed goods.

'Rising prices provoked a variety of reactions. In Hitchin, a shop was attacked and looted. In Benwell, near Newcastle, flour dealers' shops were wrecked' and there were attacks on German butchers and bakers, both on account of their nationality and of price rises.

The bank rate rose to 10%, ready cash became short and queues formed outside the Bank of England to withdraw gold. After an emergency meeting with financial leaders, the Bank Holiday was extended by three days. That night crowds sang patriotic songs outside Buckingham Palace.

On 2 August, although overcast by the threat of war and Germany's demand for passage through Belgium, most people carried on as normal. It was a holiday and people wanted a good time even though some sporting events like Cowes were cancelled. While trains took them to the seaside, trains were also taking aliens back across the channel in response to their call-up, leaving 'many hotels and restaurants suddenly bereft of their staffs.' Even the King was affected. He lost his foreign chef.

In France the reaction was once again different to that in Germany. After the declaration of war, Berlin was in a jubilant mood, its streets filled with excited, singing crowds and the bars open well into the night. By contrast, in Paris, angry crowds attacked German and Austrian shops, resulting in a curfew on cafés and restaurants and the banning of loiterers.

Tuesday, 4 August, saw the end of peace. In the Reichstag, the Kaiser justified German actions, and in Paris a political truce was announced – an Union Sacrée – and a 'state of siege' was implemented giving the government unlimited powers. Across the channel, Britain sent Germany an ultimatum that expired at eleven that night. When there was no reaction from 10 Downing Street, the waiting crowd quickly dispersed 'shouting almost hysterically "War! War! War!".'

When recruiting offices opened the next day, business was brisk. In just four days over 8,000 men enlisted. The number had grown to 100,000 by 22 August. Living in central London, Hallie Miles recorded the sight in her diary. 'We see the women bringing their men to the Recruiting Offices and waiting outside whilst they are being enlisted. The men who had entered the building in civilian clothes – working clothes, all sorts of clothes – leave it in spic and span uniform, and the women are handed their men's everyday garments.' Sometimes they wept over these as they turned away, leaving their men behind. At some offices recruits were being held back by the police and only let in in small batches.

Even before war had been declared, Territorials had been embodied and large numbers of troops started to move around the country to their war stations. Mobilisation orders further increased the number of men moving around the country, curtailing excursion trains and stranding some passengers.

'Much of Europe was thrilled by the news of war.' It would mean honours, medals and promotions. Glorious deeds would create new legends and myths. Quickly men went to the war. 'Bands played. Women wept. Rifles were studded with flowers. It was "on to Paris" and "à Berlin", "God save the tsar", and "Gott mit uns".'

With the harvest to collect, the countryside displayed less enthusiasm and not every country town was in a jubilant mood. Travelling by train from Birmingham to Dorset, on 5 August, Mary Stocks recorded crowds 'at every station, but that they were unhappy, bewildered and apprehensive.' In Portsmouth the declaration 'was greeted with shock and horror', while in Chester it was accepted enthusiastically.

There was opposition in Britain to the war: pacifists, some non-conformists and many socialists stood up for their beliefs. Generally, though most opponents kept a low profile.

'In towns across the country, the war immediately dampened sales: "shopkeepers, except those who sell provisions, are doing little trade" and at some factories and workshops short time was immediately put in place. Change was coming quickly. Bank notes for ten shillings and one pound were suddenly issued, exchangeable at the Bank of England for gold. Postal Orders became legal tender and banks were given powers to disallow the withdrawal of gold for hoarding, but cash would be available for wages and salaries and the normal cash requirements of daily life. The bank rate was reduced from ten to six per cent.'

'Further change and more governmental control arrived with the passing of what became known as DORA, the Defence of the Realm Act, on 8 August. "It gave the government wide-ranging powers during the war period, such as the power to requisition buildings or land needed for the war effort, or to make regulations creating criminal offences." It would have far-reaching effects and affect everyone. The Act was amended during the war, with some aspects of it remaining law well after the war was over, for example, pub opening hours during the day.' Effectively the act, passed in just five minutes, signed away traditional freedoms that had long been jealously prized and guarded.

Five days later details of the Act appeared in the *London Gazette*. 'The Act covered all aspects of life: "no-one was allowed to talk about naval or military matters in public places; no-one was allowed to spread rumours about military matters; no-one was allowed to buy binoculars; no-one was allowed to trespass on railway lines or bridges; no-one was allowed to melt down gold or silver; no-one was allowed to light bonfires or fireworks".' The list of prohibitions grew with each year of the war.

In Europe numbers of holidaymakers tried to get home before the war started. Many were given an unpleasant time as they left Germany, with stories of luggage being thrown out of trains and left behind. This was to some extent to be expected: with so many trains moving to the front, there was little room for civilians in any of the countries. However, their stories did make interesting reading in the local papers when they arrived home.

The initial stages of the war created huge numbers of refugees; they left with what they could carry and moved to quieter areas. In each country there were foreign nationals, Allied and enemy who had to be housed, imprisoned or sent on. Some of these might well have been spies. Scotland Yard quickly rounded up the most dangerous of the known German agents.

On both sides there was a wave of xenophobic spy-mania. Every foreigner was a possible enemy agent. 'In early August German police stations were crowded with aliens, most of them tourists caught by the outbreak of war and arrested as spies…Englishmen in particular were ill-treated… and many were sent, regardless of age or sex, to the dreaded Spandau fortress.' It was the same in Britain where the large number of Germans 'made a happy hunting ground', especially German shopkeepers, barbers and waiters. To reduce such confusion many simply changed their names. After all, they were naturalised, and Stohwasser became Stowe. Rosenheim Rose, and Schmitt Smith - the same people, different names and no problem. In Berlin, famous English designations disappeared. Hotel Westminster and Café Piccadilly became respectively Hotel Lindenhof and Vaterland. Food and dog types changed: Chauffeur became schauffoer and Dachshund became sausage dog.

There were scores of wounded who had to be dealt with. Materials had to be manufactured and moved in greater quantities than ever before. Nations were short of money or unable to provide necessities quickly, so people volunteered to help and large numbers contributed to a range of fund-raising charities. As a result of people's need to be involved, so many socks were knitted that the government had to intervene.

In Britain and Germany, volunteers had flocked to join the forces. To house these men, the displaced, and the wounded, buildings were needed. Homes were turned into hospitals and billets, schools closed and re-opened as VAD hospitals. Businesses that once turned out peaceful products switched to war production.

Many British firms gave employees a right to return to their employment after their service and offered to look after their families. This could add to the pressure to enlist, already overwhelming from countless posters and adverts in the papers. The firm of Aquascutum can be taken as a fairly typical if unusually very generous example. An August advert told readers that they issued a notice to their employees about enlisting. 'We think it is absolutely necessary for every single man between nineteen and thirty to answer his country's call. We shall be pleased to pay half his present salary to any one of our present employees while serving and will keep his situation open for him on his return. In the event of a parent or parents being dependent on the volunteer, full salary will be paid him during his service.' Further pressure came from the names of volunteers printed in local papers each week.

As a result of such pressure, some schools lacked male teachers. Farmers had problems harvesting, although many agricultural labourers waited until the crops were in and their contracts had finished for the year. The same was not true for their horses. 'Parties of soldiers descended and led away their stock to the mustering grounds, sometimes illegally and to the detriment of the harvest.' Prices for potential cavalry horses were £75 for an officer's charger, but most animals were needed for transport. Across the country, village greens and parks were ad hoc trading grounds. At the Tower of London the moat was filled with horses.

Naturally such changes affected women. In France they took over the farms left by men gone to the front, while in the towns they enrolled for nursing. In Britain women volunteered to run canteens, provide troop comforts and nurse. 'Germany's enlistment of women was the most far-reaching and efficient of all.' Women manned the trams of Berlin from the first days of the war. By the end of September they were making bread sacks, ammunition belts and other essentials. Thousands were sent to work on farms and in army equipment factories.

In Britain there was intense concern about a German invasion among both the military and civilians. This 'prompted many civilians to enlist in local rifle clubs' and join non-military sanctioned defence units. Although Britain was an island, the German navy was large and the German lines were close to Calais and Boulogne. Civilians were to stay at home in the event of an invasion unless told to move. Beaches were covered in barbed wire. Trenches were dug along cliffs, pleasure piers rendered unusable, scouts guarded bridges and tunnels and some Sea Scouts, the pick of the best, were given coastguard cottages were they cooked and cleaned for themselves and went out looking for suspicious ships, planes or people. In the event of an invasion anything that might be useful to an invader was to be destroyed or rendered useless.

Destruction by shell and bomb were not confined to other fronts. German ships shelled coastal towns and Zeppelins bombed towns and cities across England. Civilians experienced 'blackout', and unlit roads resulted in traffic fatalities. However, while shell and bomb killed, and people knew this was a possible danger, it was for most, extremely unlikely.

In Britain, alarming stories appeared in the papers because press censorship was not as stringent as in France or Germany, nor was it controlled by the military. Although the Press Bureau issued the official news and censored independent stories, papers did not have to submit editorial copy to them. However, they could be prosecuted under DORA for publishing restricted 'military information as well as false statements regarding the war. This was a strong incentive to get preliminary clearance from the Bureau.' However, there was no censorship of opinion or of stories or letters from the front, as long as they made no mention of place. As a result, many quite disturbing pieces appeared in local papers.

This was different to the situation in both France and Germany. Military news was restricted to bare statements in Germany, and, on non-military matters, editors were told what could or could not be written. There was no free expression at home and foreign correspondents were provided with propaganda by the Foreign Office. Like the Germans, the French press was also under military control that restricted war news to official communiqués, banned big headlines and vendors shouting their wares, and limited papers to one edition a day.

The war did have a positive side. It banished internal differences and united 'dissenting elements in a bond of loyalty: in face of the danger without, party conflicts were shelved and current political issues put aside.' This was achieved in Britain, France and Germany against a 'background of profound social change and ferment, even instability.' Britain's problems included Ireland, women's rights, poverty, trade union unrest and class inequalities. In France there had been social and labour unrest, party conflicts, disordered government finances and anti-militarist feeling. The booming German economy had helped reduce discontent but the Social Democrats had campaigned for democratic reform, new suffrage laws and relief from Prussian militarism. All was forgotten. There was a war to be won.

Very quickly it was Christmas. On both sides it was a time of seasonal gaiety mixed with austerity: 'Your present must be something useful this time.' Generally, there was no shortage of goods, although some things were more difficult to get hold of than others.

The real shortage was money to buy the requisites needed for the man or animal at the front or the refugee. Many ingenious methods of getting money out of the public were used, the most common being the Flag Day, of which there were many every year.

The same feelings were experienced in towns and cities in war-torn Europe. There was a commonality of experience between the warring nations, which, importantly, gave many Europeans a sense of purpose. This is their experience in pictorial form.

Section One:
The pre-war world

157 M. PARIS — La grande roue

GWHF14_001. The Grande Roue de Paris was a 100-metre (328 ft) tall Ferris wheel built for the 1900 Exposition Universelle world exhibition at Paris. It was the tallest wheel in the world at the time of its opening. The passenger cars were so large that they were removed from the wheel and used as homes for French families from devastated regions during the war.

GWHF14_005. Emphasising the links between the European Royal Famili[es] this is a picture of the Prince of Wal[es] on a visit to Germany before the war He travelled as the Earl of Chester accompanied by his equerry, William Cadogan, son of Earl Cadogan. Cadogan was killed in action on 12 November 1914 commanding the 10t[h] Hussars.

GWHF14_002. A symbol of British prosperity, the Royal Exchange.

GWHF14_003. Berlin was equally prosperous and much more spacious. This is Potsdam Square in the centre of the city.

GWHF14_009. British battleships in line during the 1914 review attended by the King. A strong message to the world of Britain's strength

GWHF14_012. In order to keep troops fully trained and ready, armies have always held manoeuvres to practise attack and defence on a large scale. This picture was taken during German Army manoeuvres in 1913.

GWHF14_016. With a large conscript army, the French also held full-scale manoeuvres in 1913. Here troops are resting during the lunch break.

GWHF14_015. Austrian officers saluting their empire and emperor.

GWHF14_017. German troops in 1912 who are just coming to the end of their training. They were transfered to the reserve and called up in August 1914 for service.

GWHF14_020. Britain had a small but well-trained regular army. Here are some men at the Soldiers' Christian Association at Olympia.

GWHF14_019. In Britain the summer meant a week in camp for most of Britain's part-time soldiers, the Territorials. This is a battalion of the Middlesex Regiment at camp in 1913.

GWHF14_030. Any excuse for a parade. With no government provision for health care, money had to be raised voluntarily to fund hospitals. This is a charity parade, jointly held by members of the church and chapel in Spencer's Wood, for the Royal Berkshire Hospital.

GWHF14_032. Demonstrating their excellent stature and physique, boys from the Wellington College, many of whom will, within weeks, be officers in the army, demonstrate physical drill during the annual Speech Day.

GWHF14_038. The Kaiser and the King were closely related, as were many German and British families. This photo was sent from Willi, in full uniform, to his cousins in London, asking why they had not been in contact.

GWHF14_033. At Wellington College there was the annual Speech Day with events. Here, parents are resting after the speeches, eating strawberries and cream.

GWHF14_040. On the Alsace frontier French and German troops faced each other but usually not in such numbers or close. The reason for this photo is unknown.

GWHF14_031. In France people were more interested in the trial of Henriette Caillaux than the threat of war. She had shot and killed Gaston Calmette, editor of *'Le Figaro'*, to stop him publishing intimate letters that would destroy her husband's career as Minister of Finance. Her attorney 'convinced the jury that her crime, which she did not deny, was not a premeditated act but that her uncontrollable female emotions resulted in a crime of passion. The belief that women were not as strong emotionally as men resulted in her acquittal on 28 July 1914.'

GWHF14_042. Gun runners, during the Irish Troubles, at Howth, Ireland, during July 1914.

GWHF14_037. Members of a German patriotic organisation on a trip only days before the mobilisation order would see them called to the colours.

Section Two:
Mobilisation, recruiting and departure

GWHF14_048. With Germany mobilising, hundreds of young Germans living in Britain went to the German Consulate for further instructions.

GWHF14_049. While Europe was mobilising, Britain, still not involved, closed the Stock Exchange because of the crisis in Europe. This crowd is in Throgmorton Street.

GWHF14_050. The crowd outside a Paris bank on news of mobilisation.

GWHF14_053. An orderly queue outside the bank of England during the period leading to mobilisation.

GWHF14_054. A similar scene outside the Bank of France during the crisis.

Ansprache des Kaisers an sein Volk
am Freitag den 31. Juli 1914.

Kr.2
Verlag von
A.V. LIERSCH & Cº
BERLIN S.W.

Bremer phot.

„Der Kaiser spricht."

Eine schwereStunde ist heute über Deutschland hereingebrochen. Neider überall zwingen uns zu gerechter Verteidigung. Man drückt uns das Schwert in die Hand. Ich hoffe daß, wenn es nicht in letzter Stunde meinen Bemühungen gelingt, die Gegner zum Einsehen zu bringen und den Frieden zu erhalten, wir das Schwert mit Gottes Hilfe so führen werden, daß wir es mit Ehren wieder in die Scheide stecken können. Enorme Opfer an Gut und Blut würde ein Krieg vom deutschen Volk erfordern. Den Gegnern aber würden wir zeigen, was es heißt, Deutschland anzugreifen. Und nun empfehle ich Euch Gott! Jetzt geht in die Kirche, kniet nieder vor Gott und bittet ihn um Hilfe für unser braves Heer!"

GWHF14_055. On 31 July the Kaiser spoke from the balcony of the Royal Palace: 'A momentous hour has struck Germany...the sword has been forced into our hands...we may use the sword...we shall show the enemy what it means to attack Germany'.

GWHF14_057. Reading the mobilisation orders that were posted on civic buildings across Germany.

GWHF14_058. Contrary to German belief, the order to mobilise was carried out quickly. Here a Russian reservist says goodbye to his family.

GWHF14_059. French mobilisation orders went up at almost the same time as those in Germany. Here French citizens read the newly posted orders.

ARMÉE DE TERRE ET ARMÉE DE MER

ORDRE DE MOBILISATION GÉNÉRALE

Par décret du Président de la République, la mobilisation des armées de terre et de mer est ordonnée, ainsi que la réquisition des animaux, voitures et harnais nécessaires au complément de ces armées.

Le premier jour de la mobilisation est le dimanche deux août 1914

Tout Français soumis aux obligations militaires doit, sous peine d'être puni avec toute la rigueur des lois, obéir aux prescriptions du **FASCICULE DE MOBILISATION** (pages coloriées placées dans son livret).

Sont visés par le présent ordre **TOUS LES HOMMES** non présents sous les Drapeaux et appartenant :

1° à l'**ARMÉE DE TERRE** y compris les **TROUPES COLONIALES** et les hommes des **SERVICES AUXILIAIRES**;

2° à l'**ARMÉE DE MER** y compris les **INSCRITS MARITIMES** et les **ARMURIERS** de la **MARINE**.

Les Autorités civiles et militaires sont responsables de l'exécution du présent décret.

Le Ministre de la Guerre.　　　　　　*Le Ministre de la Marine.*

GWHF14_060. The French mobilisation order was posted on Saturday 1 August to take effect the next day. Many set off early and arrived at depots before it had officially begun.

GWHF14_061. German reservists on their way to their call-up depot in Berlin, accompanied by their children. Note the children's lack of footwear.

GWHF14_062. Regular troops quickly moved to their war stations on mobilisation. Here Austrian troops are marching through the city centre to the railway station.

GWHF14_063. Newly called-up German reservists, still in civilian clothes, wait for transport to take them to their kaserne (barracks).

GWHF14_066. French reservists arriving in Paris from outlying regions.

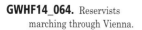

GWHF14_064. Reservists marching through Vienna.

GWHF14_065. Many of the newly mobilised men had a last photo taken as a keep-sake for relatives. This is a French cavalry officer's picture, sent to his family just after mobilisation.

[Form to be used when the whole of the Army Reserve is called out.]

Army Form D. 427.

GENERAL MOBILIZATION
Army Reserve
(REGULAR AND SPECIAL RESERVISTS).

HIS MAJESTY THE KING has been graciously pleased to direct by Proclamation that the Army Reserve be called out on permanent service.

ALL REGULAR RESERVISTS are required to report themselves at once at their place of joining in accordance with the instructions on their identity certificates for the purpose of joining the Army.

ALL SPECIAL RESERVISTS are required to report themselves on such date and at such places as they may be directed to attend for the purpose of joining the Army. If they have not received any such directions, or if they have changed their address since last attendance at drill or training, they will report themselves at once, by letter, to the Adjutant of their Unit or Depot.

The necessary instructions as to their joining will then be given.

4514 100,000 11—11 Forms D. 427.
8 14 55 11

Printed for H. M. Stationery Office by HAZELL, WATSON & VINEY, LD., 52, Long Acre, London, W.C.

GWHF14_076. A poster proclaiming the general mobilisation of the Army reserve.

GWHF14_068. German naval reservists arriving at the dock prior to being taken to their ship.

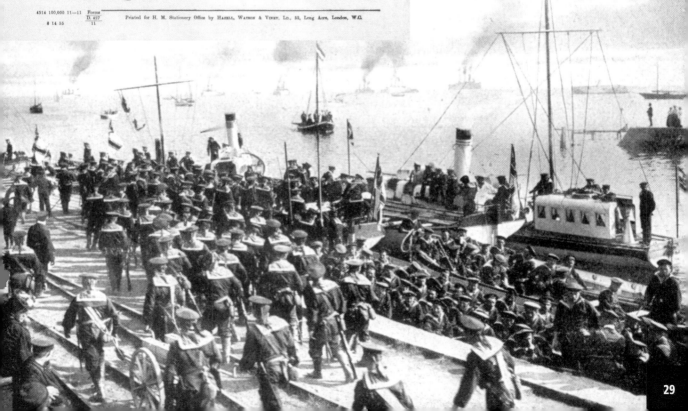

GWHF14_078. A Gloucestershire Regiment Territorial who volunteered for overseas service.

GWHF14_077. General mobilisation was for both branches of the service. Before leaving for their stations and depots many men had their photo taken professionally. This is a Royal Naval Reservist.

GWHF14_075. Crowds outside the Feldherrnhalle, in Munich, on 2 August when mobilisation commenced.

GWHF14_079. A young German officer poses with his family before leaving for the front.

GWHF14_081. Three brothers and the family dog pose for perhaps the last time together. On the left is a Royal Navy Petty Officer with three good conduct badges, in the centre is a RAMC private and on the right is a Leading Seaman with two good conduct badges serving in the Royal Flying Corps naval branch.

GWHF14_083. A German officer reads the declaration of war to the crowd.

GWHF14_091. Berlin crowds cheering the war.

GWHF14_084. Jubilant crowds in Berlin on the declaration of war.

GWHF14_087. Patriotic gathering for troops in Vienna.

GWHF14_092. In front of the Royal Palace, in Berlin, on the declaration of war.

GWHF14_094. The crowds in Vienna on the declaration of war.

GWHF14_095. The scene in front of Buckingham Palace as war was announced.

AUGUST 5, 1914.

BRITAIN AT WAR

GWHF14_096. The next day newspaper hoardings told the public of the decision for war. This from *The Times* is straightforward.

GWHF14_099. A more restrained crowd read the declaration of war in Budapest.

GWHF14_098. In Paris crowds of men marched through the city holding French and British flags.

GWHF14_106. In France, the sudden declaration found many holidaymakers stranded. This is the queue outside the British Consulate.

GWHF14_102. When street lamps started to be dimmed or reduced in number it became necessary to paint kerbs white so they could be seen in the dark.

GWHF14_105. In a state of war, many public buildings in London were guarded by the military. This is Somerset House.

GWHF14_108. In cities across Germany, private cars suddenly became transport for the wounded, driven by their owners.

GWHF14_113. France resented her loss of Alsace and Lorraine to the Germans in 1871. On state occasions the Strasbourg monument was covered in black and at other times was decorated with wreaths. This practice did not end until France regained the region after the war. This is a Patriotic demonstration around the Strassbourg statue in Paris when French troops entered Alsace.

GWHF14_115. Austrian cadets display their enthusiasm on the declaration of war. 'After being sworn in, the Austrian "sucklings," or cadets, were drawn up in a square, where they gave a loud "Hochs!" for their Kaiser as they uplifted their un-fleshed swords high in the air.'

GWHF14_126. Within days of mobilisation regular troops moved to their port of embarkation.

GWHF14_125. Territorial units were sent to train in, and guard, parts of the country they were not familiar with. F Company of 5th Cheshire Regiment were from Chester and on mobilisation moved to Shrewsbury and then to Northampton, where this photo was taken at the end of August.

GWHF14_128. Men of 5th Royal Scots Fusiliers on their way to Stirling from Kilmarnock in August 1914.

GWHF14_129. Men were mobilised and vehicles commandeered. These are civilian vehicles parked in Hyde Park waiting for their new owners to take them away. Private motorists and large firms surrendered vehicles in great numbers to the government. On August 5, the 'Chief Metropolitan Police Magistrate, Sir John Dickinson, was all day busy signing warrants authorising the commandeering, not only of motor-vehicles, but of horses, petrol, and other things required by the Government for the national defence. As each warrant was signed, it was taken away by two Army officers attended by a sergeant of the police.' Cars were taken whether the owner agreed to the price or not but they did have the right of appeal in court afterwards.

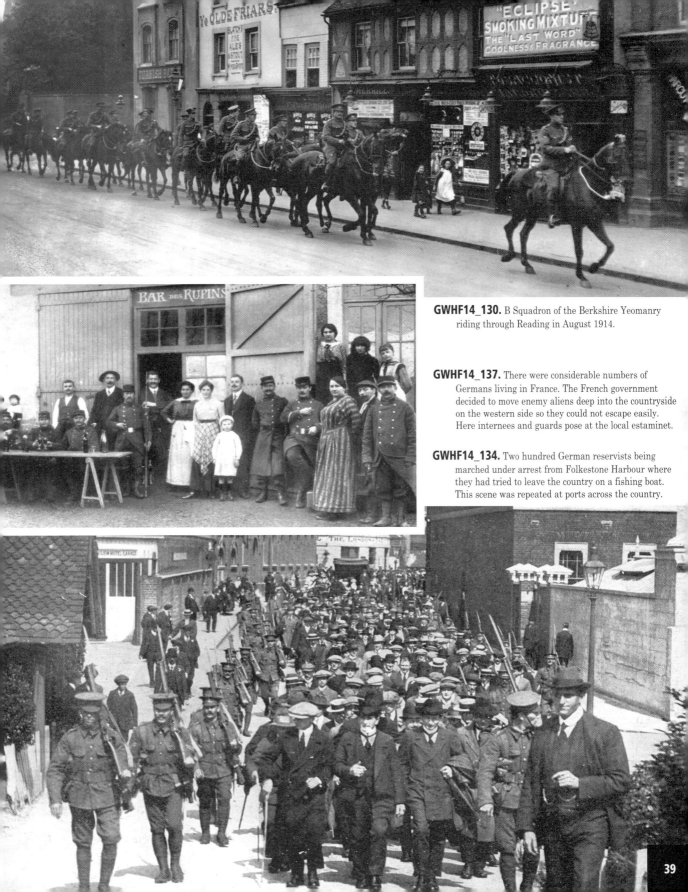

GWHF14_130. B Squadron of the Berkshire Yeomanry riding through Reading in August 1914.

GWHF14_137. There were considerable numbers of Germans living in France. The French government decided to move enemy aliens deep into the countryside on the western side so they could not escape easily. Here internees and guards pose at the local estaminet.

GWHF14_134. Two hundred German reservists being marched under arrest from Folkestone Harbour where they had tried to leave the country on a fishing boat. This scene was repeated at ports across the country.

GWHF14_138. A disused factory in France converted into a hostel for young female Germans.

GWHF14_145. There was no appeal for volunteers in Germany because it had a conscript army. However, the yearly call-up did not take all eligible males and at the start of the war thousands of men who had not been conscripted, volunteered, many of them students. CAs in Britain, their accommodation was initially temporary.

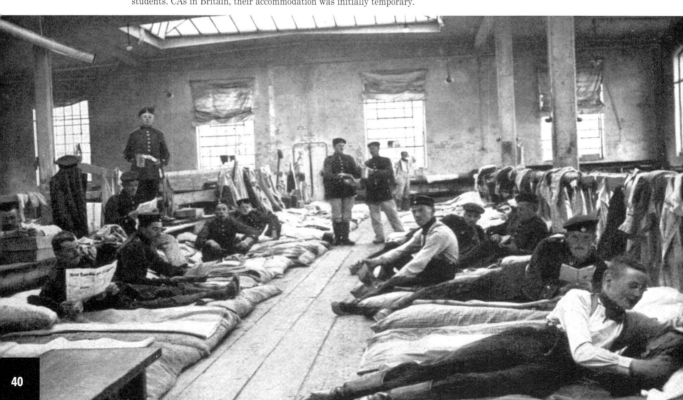

Your King and Country Need You!

A CALL TO ARMS!

An addition of 100,000 men to His Majesty's Regular Army is immediately necessary in the present grave National Emergency. Lord Kitchener is confident that this appeal will be at once responded to by all those who have the safety of our Empire at heart.

TERMS OF SERVICE:
General Service for a period of 3 years or until the War is concluded.
Age of Enlistment between 19 and 30.

HOW TO JOIN.
Full information can be obtained at any Post Office in the United Kingdom or at any Military Depot.

God Save the King.

GWHF14_147. America may have been neutral but this did not stop them joining in. Many crossed the border into Canada to enlist while some, resident in other countries, joined that nation's forces. These are American volunteers for the French Army.

GWHF14_141. Within days, Kitchener, realising that the BEF was not big enough, called for more men.

GWHF14_148. Martial music was a good method of stimulating interest and patriotism. Here recruits follow the drummers after they have just enlisted on Horse Guards Parade.

GWHF14_149. Waiting to enlist outside Whitehall.

GWHF14_150. A street procession to encourage those who hesitated to join.

GWHF14_159. Another method of recruiting was a free concert. This one was held in Regent Street.

GWHF14_152. The need for more men is shown in this poster. Certain selected ex-NCOs up to the age of 50 could enlist because of the numbers of men in training and the shortage of trained NCOs. They would not accompany their men abroad because they were too old.

GWHF14_153. The Central London Recruiting Depot besieged by men wanting to enlist.

GWHF14_161. A recruit pledging allegiance.

GWHF14_156. Women were powerful recruiting officers. The sign reads 'SERVE YOUR COUNTRY OR WEAR THIS.'

GWHF14_169. Old soldiers were also recruited to help increase enlistment.

GWHF14_166. Central Recruiting in London on a busy day.

GWHF14_163. Recruits enjoying a hearty meal. In many cases they were eating better than in civilian life.

GWHF14_170. A London store doing its bit for recruitment.

GWHF14_171. William Wood, an eighty-two-year-old artilleryman who fought in the Crimea and the Indian Mutiny, acted as an amateur recruiting officer in the villages outside Reading.

FOR THE GLORY OF IRELAND

BELGIUM

'WILL YOU GO OR MUST I'?

GWHF14_175. Women as recruiters: this is to protect her and Ireland.

O.H.M.S.

WANTED,

1,000 Athletes

AND OTHER FOLLOWERS OF SPORT.

ECRUITING NOW PROCEEDING

FOR THE

3rd HULL (SERVICE) BATTALION
EAST YORKSHIRE REGIMENT.

f you mean to Play the Game

JOIN AT ONCE.

CITY HALL,

Open Daily 10 to 10.

GWHF14_179. A further method to stimulate recruiting was to create battalions where men would feel at home. These were usually known as Pals battalions.

GWHF14_187. Troops marching through Paris. The one onlooker does not look too happy about the situation.

GWHF14_186. Once kitted out, reservists were liable for front-line service. These men, only days after reporting, are leaving Paris for the front.

GWHF14_189. For many of the men, this was their first experience of city life.

GWHF14_190. To release trained men, the Garde Civile took over guarding sensitive areas across France in the same way as the Territorials, Scouts and Special Constables did in Britain.

GWHF14_193. German soldiers prior to leaving for the front.

GWHF14_191. Men who had left their villages in the south of France quickly found themselves defending similar villages in the north. These men were serving with the 140th Territorial Regiment in the north of France.

GWHF14_194. Possibly a final photo. A German officer and his wife solemnly pose for the photographer.

GWHF14_196. A reservist poses for the family album just before catching the train to the front.

GWHF14_195. A rather (un)caring final photo, for a husband leaving for the front.

GWHF14_203. The Kaiser and his entourage at the mobilisation of the 1st Foot Guard Regiment.

GWHF14_197. A youthful rating ready to take his place on SMS *Hannover*, a Deutschland class, pre-Dreadnought. This ship was sent to guard the Elbe River during the fleet mobilisation.

GWHF14_199. Father and son, both officers, ready to leave.

GWHF14_206. The start of the journey for a naval detachment at the onset of mobilisation.

GWHF14_208. In the early days of the war, it was common for departing men to be given flowers to attach to their uniform.

GWHF14_207. Reservist being given a lift to the collection point by a friendly lorry driver.

GWHF14_209. As well as receiving flowers, departing men were often escorted by members of their families to the railway station.

GWHF14_210. Checking and helping each other put on their equipment before the march to the station.

GWHF14_211. All over the country, columns of men made their way to the station. These are Bavarian Landwehr marching through Munich.

GWHF14_212. A Kurassier regiment is being waved off enthusiastically.

GWHF14_213. Taken in Berlin in August 1914, this photo shows a mother giving something to her son as he leaves for the front. Not all departures were seen off by large crowds. Note that the soldier wearing a Red Cross armband is carrying a rifle.

GWHF14_214. When the war volunteers were trained, they took their place at the front. Here they are leaving Berlin on 30 November to an enthusiastic send-off.

GWHF14_215. An Austrian infantry regiment marching through Linz on the way to the station.

GWHF14_218. A scene repeated across Europe: wives saying goodbye to their husbands. This photo was taken in Austria.

GWHF14_216. The same scene in Hungary. Landwehr starting for the front.

GWHF14_219. A Hungarian Honved infantry regiment's flag being blessed before leaving for the front.

GWHF14_222. The Black Watch leaving Aldershot for the front. As regular soldiers they were a considerable distance from their families so did not get the same send-off as their German equivalents. A hundred years earlier they had just returned from Spain where they had been fighting against the French.

GWHF14_221. The commandant of Jaffa watches Turkish troops marching through to the front.

GWHF14_220. Commander-in-chief of Turkish troops in Palestine walking through Jerusalem.

GWHF14_226. The first Tasmanian contingent leaving Hobart.

GWHF14_225. Royal Grenadiers entraining at Montreal.

GWHF14_224. Troops leaving Canada on 10 October aboard the SS *Scandinavian*.

GWHF14_231. Austrian troops being seen off from the sidings to shouts of Hurra! Hurra! Hurra!

GWHF14_233. Austrian troops leaving Vienna for the Eastern Front.

GWHF14_232. Honved troops leaving for the Galician front.

GWHF14_240. German reservists being sent off to the sounds of martial music. The original caption told of them going off to a Holy War.

GWHF14_236. Older reservists, Landsturm, leaving Berlin for training camps. Even they felt the need to write down the eventual destination of their train. Once ag it was Paris.

GWHF14_235. With so many troops leaving for the front, most had to settle for trucks rather than passenger cars.

GWHF14_241. A propaganda photo purporting to show the oldest man going off to fight. Again his destination is Paris.

GWHF14_244. Scenes of wild enthusiasm and rejoicing met the news that the forts at Liège were holding up the German advance.

GWHF14_245. Crowds gathering in Vienna to hear the latest news from the front.

GWHF14_248. Across the continent men marched to take up their war stations or get to the front. Here, either the 4th or 5th battalion of the Royal Welsh Fusiliers march towards Northampton in late August.

GWHF14_247. The French Home Front saw a rapid influx of men of all nations. Here newly arrived members of the BEF are greeted on the quayside at Boulogne. They were under orders to behave well.

GWHF14_249. The North Midland Division, Royal Engineers Signal Company pose after their successful move to Luton.

Section Three:
Getting ready for war

GWHF14_253. The embodiment order for the London Territorials was received on 4 August, before war was declared. Within twelve hours every member of the force in London had been summoned by letter and before noon next day 40,000 had been mobilised. The sixty vacancies in the London Scottish were filled immediately.

GWHF14_254. The Royal Family showed great interest in all military matters throughout the war but took a particular interest in the Grenadier Guards. This photo was taken just after the Prince of Wales had joined them as a Second Lieutenant and as the battalion left for France.

GWHF14_255. As the younger men went off to war, older men wanted to assist in any way possible. Thousands formed their own defence companies to assist the army although it would quite some while before they were officially recognised. Here some over-age volunteers are being inspected.

GWHF14_257. While most troops would be needed at the front, many held other jobs. Two marines patrol the Bodensee, the border between Germany, Austria and Switzerland, making sure no contraband is moved across the lake.

GWHF14_256. When men enlisted and moved to depots or away from home, their wives became entitled to a separation allowance. Here women queue for the weekly payment.

GWHF14_258. On the German-Swiss border between Konstanz and Kreuzlingen, two Swiss civilians are having their papers checked by German Landsturm border guards.

GWHF14_261. These Austro-Hungarian soldiers are guarding a railway bridge on the Serbian border.

GWHF14_260. Imaginations ran amok with stories of spies and espionage. As a result of the imagined threats, bridges everywhere were guarded. This French soldier guards a bridge at St. Denis.

GWHF14_262. A damaged tunnel would hinder the flow of material to the front. Here a mountain tunnel in Austria is being guarded. There were men at both ends to secure its safety.

GWHF14_263. In Germany, the Landsturm provided men to watch over sensitive areas. This is the bridge watch for the town of Speyer on the River Rhine. Judging by the bottles they are not expecting sabotage.

GWHF14_264. Dress uniforms were quickly replaced by khaki when the war started. This is a Grenadier Guard on duty at Buckingham Palace.

GWHF14_266. In this picture men from Lancashire are guarding a railway siding in Reading.

GWHF14_268. For those territorials not yet ready for the front, an essential task was to defend Britain's long coastline against possible invasion. This is a field artillery detachment guarding the Withernsea coast in December 1914.

GWHF14_270. The East Anglian coastline was a possible invasion area and was heavily guarded by territorials and troops in training. These are Essex cyclists patrolling a coast road in Essex.

GWHF14_269. The Guernsey Militia marching off after parade. They were tasked with guarding the island from invasion.

GWHF14_272. Territorials guarding the cable station at Cunard Bay on the Isle of Wight. According to Admiral Jellicoe, it was the safest place in the world.

GWHF14_275. On look-out from a splinter proof trench on the East Coast.

GWHF14_278. Men of the Royal Naval Division in training at Crystal Palace, Sydenham.

GWHF14_280. Part of the continuous flow of troops from Australia. A Victorian contingent marching through Melbourne prior to leaving Australia.

GWHF14_286. The question asked at the time was whether they would match the C.I.V.s of the Boer War period: newly raised Territorials marching along the Strand.

GWHF14_290. The 2nd Battalion Grenadier Guards march past the King outside Buckingham Palace. On the left are Princess Victoria, the Prince of Wales and Princess Mary. Also present are Queen Alexandra, Queen Mary and Princess Christian.

GWHF14_287. Canadian Highlanders marching through London.

GWHF14_289. At Bustard Camp on Salisbury Plain, men of the PPCLI (Princess Patricia's Canadian Light Infantry) with their colours. These had been worked by Princess Patricia.

GWHF14_291. The 2nd City Battalion of the Liverpool Regiment arriving at Hooton racecourse in October.

GWHF14_293. Australian cadets being inspected by Lord Kitchener at Bisley.

GWHF14_298. The King leaving Bustard Camp, Salisbury Plain, after inspecting Canadian troops on 4 November.

GWHF14_299. The King and Queen during their inspection of Canadian troops on Salisbury Plain.

GWHF14_304. Scottish volunteers with a machine gun on a carriage.

GWHF14_305. A novel sight in the city: buildings under guard by Indian troops.

GWHF14_309. Field church service in the courtyard of the Weimar Palace held before the 1st battalion, 94th (5th Thuringian) Infantry "Grand Duke of Saxony" Regiment, left for the front in August.

GWHF14_325. A shortage of khaki meant that new recruits wore their own clothes: a mixture of their own clothes and some uniform. As a stop-gap, many were issued with a blue uniform like this member of a Lancashire Fusiliers battalion.

GWHF14_327. A photo that clearly shows the situation in which many new volunteers found themselves. These recruits are lucky: they have a rifle and one, at least, has some form of uniform.

GWHF14_326. A Cheshire Battalion, wearing the blue uniform, proudly display the few rifles they possess.

GWHF14_334. As the German Army was normally much bigger than the British Army, more space was available. All the same, there were still many thousands of men in training. These are learning bayonet fighting.

GWHF14_328. Concerns about inebriation were unfounded. Newspaper reports showed that there was no real increase in drunkenness when soldiers were in the area. Again, this picture clearly shows the shortage of uniform.

GWHF14_335. Canadian troops training on the rifle butts at Valcartier army base, north of Quebec. They are using the Ross rifle which was very accurate but prone to jamming when faced with the mud on the Western Front.

GWHF14_337. There were many British and Americans living in France at the start of the war. These British volunteers for the French Army are undergoing drill.

GWHF14_336. German troops learning to climb fences, how much use such training was in the confined spaces of the trenches is unclear but it undoubtedly made them fit.

GWHF14_338. Freiwillige soldiers, the equivalent of Kitchener's Army, undergoing training. Like their British counterparts, they had many reasons for volunteering for active service. They were all men who had not been included in the annual conscription. Unlike their British counterparts there was no shortage of uniforms.

GWHF14_344. Although it was not used as much as is generally believed, the bayonet was a frightening weapon. It was essential that a soldier was proficient in its use.

GWHF14_339. German troops under training.

GWHF14_346. Territorial units were almost fully equipped before the war but they were not fully trained. This is the North Midland Field Ambulance undergoing training in Wiltshire.

GWHF14_348. Infantry training in stealth attacks: a skill not much used in the early stages of the war. With the most modern weapons needed at the front, they are training with an obsolete rifle.

GWHF14_354. The British Army also raised battalions from overseas recruits. These are men of the 2nd King Edward's Horse drilling at White City. The regiment was organised by Major Norton Griffiths.

GWHF14_350. A battalion parading near the sea front in a mixture of their own clothes and the emergency blue uniform.

GWHF14_357. An elderly militiaman guarding an underpass in Munich.

GWHF14_359. Enthusiastic recruits drilling in Hyde Park.

GWHF14_363. Training on a 60-pounder which had seen service in the Boer War. It had an effective range of seven miles.

GWHF14_364. A group of four photos showing the Queen Victoria Rifles exercising, using street railings for Swedish Drill, near Jack Straw's Castle at Hampstead.

GWHF14_365. The exhibition grounds of the White City at Shepherd's Bush were taken over by the military. Some of the large show-cases were fitted out for sleeping and the grounds were used for training. The Devil's Cave makes a striking background to a unit learning drill.

GWHF14_369. German volunteers in training. There was no shortage of uniform or equipment as in Britain.

GWHF14_370. The North Midland Field Ambulance, now fully trained, waited for the casualties to arrive from France and Belgium. It was a very mobile unit and was to serve in a number of areas before the war finished. It was never sent overseas.

GWHF14_372. Billeting soldiers on families was a short-term measure before new camps could be built. This is an early camp under construction on Salisbury Plain.

GWHF14_375. Fortunately the British Empire was vast so there was plenty of space for troop training. This is the Victoria contingent in camp near Melbourne.

GWHF14_377. At the Dutch frontier, behind a barrier of barbed wire and revolving spikes.

GWHF14_373. Once the new camps were built men could move in. They now had their own barracks but did not necessarily have a weapon or a uniform.

GWHF14_379. The regimental mascot has always had a place in the British Army. This white goat was given by the King from his Cashmere herd. It was sent from Windsor to Newtown in Montgomeryshire where the 7th (Reserve) Royal Welsh Fusiliers were in training. On the left are Lady Magdalen Herbert, sister of the Earl of Powis, and the Earl's young daughter, Lady Hermione Herbert. On the right are Captains J. H. Addie and Oswald Davies.

GWHF14_380. Large numbers of troops on the move meant huge numbers of letters, postcards and parcels for the postal system to deal with. This is a German field post collection point in Berlin, manned partly by civilian personnel.

GWHF14_382. Money was also raised for men at the front. A popular game was football and there were constant requests in local papers for items like footballs.

GWHF14_384. Two war-time German volunteers ready to leave for the front.

Section Four:
Wartime life

GWHF14_388. On guard at the Dutch frontier. On the left are German troops and, on the right, two Dutch infantrymen beside their roughly-made sentry-box. Though the population of Holland was less than London, they put 400,000 men under arms.

GWHF14_387. The audience in the Guildhall cheering after Mr Asquith's patriotic speech on 4 September. 'We want first of all men, and we shall endeavour to secure that men desiring to serve together shall, wherever possible, be allotted to the same regiment or corps. The raising of battalions like county and municipal battalions with this object will be in every way encouraged.'

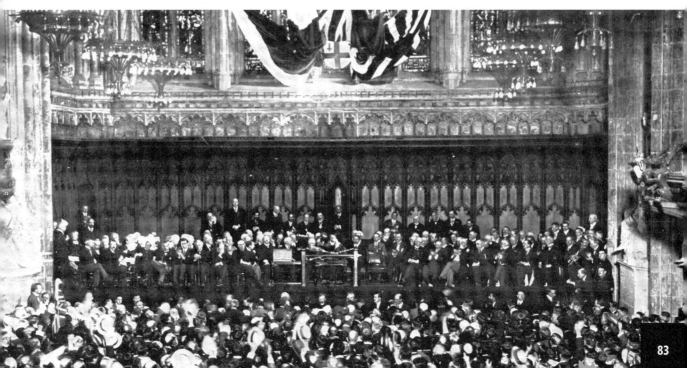

GWHF14_390. Even though neutral, Switzerland mobilised her armed forces. This is war postcard two with twenty-five percent of the price going to the Red Cross.

GWHF14_394. A young soldier, who would be old enough for the next war, has borrowed his father's equipment.

GWHF14_391. Guarding the Swiss border somewhere in the mountains.

GWHF14_416. Crowds collecting outside Hamburg city hall listening to the announcement of a further victory.

GWHF14_417. These are East Prussian refugees being handed clothing. They had fled their homes when the Russians invaded and ended up in camps near Berlin.

GWHF14_423. Making sure German refugee children are adequately fed: a Berlin food kitchen

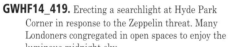

GWHF14_428. An even more unusual sight was the arrival of Indian troops. These are Hindu troops on their way to the front.

GWHF14_425. French crowds watch an unusual sight: Algerian troops marching to the front in their North-African uniform.

GWHF14_419. Erecting a searchlight at Hyde Park Corner in response to the Zeppelin threat. Many Londoners congregated in open spaces to enjoy the luminous midnight sky.

GWHF14_433. Relatives wanting information about their wounded menfolk.

5. - *Le Conflit Européen de 1914*
ANGERS - Royal's Higlanders - Une Paire Joyeuse
A HAPPY PAIR

GWHF14_431. Unusual in England as well as France were the Indian troops. Here the King is visiting wounded Indians at a hospital set up in the New Forest.

GWHF14_429. Then there were men in skirts. Two Scottish soldiers pose for the postcard photographer shortly after landing.

GWHF14_434. Reading the latest proclamation from the government.

GWHF14_441. A long with financial collections, a German newspaper ran a meat collection for the troops. The photo shows mounds of preserved meat-stuffs ready to send to the men at the front.

GWHF14_438. Not everyone wanted to be on the river. This is a works outing heading out into the Berkshire countryside.

GWHF14_437. A party embarking at Caversham Bridge in Reading for their annual works outing on the Thames.

GWHF14_442. Men and women exchanging their gold wedding rings for one made of iron, stamped 'Wilhelm II'. The gold was to be used by the government to aid the war effort.

GWHF14_444. Some of the money raised by the German Red Cross was used to provide warm underwear.

GWHF14_445. Books were always welcome at the front, and in training, to help relieve boredom. By 30 September, the German Poetry Foundation had distributed over 25,000 volumes.

GWHF14_446. Food parcels in Berlin ready for shipping.

GWHF14_447. War donations were used to buy books directly from the book trade.

GWHF14_448. There was a shortage of dressings for the wounded but no shortage of cloth to make them. In the King of Bavaria's Munich palace, society women are making various types and sizes of dressings.

GWHF14_450. With many of the postal workers at the front, their positions were taken by women. At a major sorting office in Berlin, women sort mail for the men at the front.

GWHF14_453. Making foot wraps for the Royal Grenadiers.

GWHF14_454. Everywhere horses, like men, were mobilised. Here a German monk brings the abbey's horses in for inspection.

GWHF14_458. High school students replaced the men at the front, overseen by men too old to fight.

GWHF14_456. Horse mobilisation in Hamburg in August.

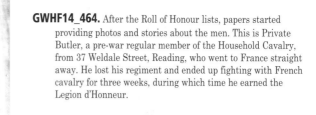

GWHF14_464. After the Roll of Honour lists, papers started providing photos and stories about the men. This is Private Butler, a pre-war regular member of the Household Cavalry, from 37 Weldale Street, Reading, who went to France straight away. He lost his regiment and ended up fighting with French cavalry for three weeks, during which time he earned the Legion d'Honneur.

GWHF14_465. Lucky escapes or strange mistakes made popular reading in local papers. 'Still smiling! Pte. B. E. Howarth, of 72, Queen's Road, Caversham, who was with the R.M.L.I. at Antwerp when the town fell.' He was reported killed by Private Bassett. On reading of his death he wrote home to tell everyone he was 'quite safe and that "someone must have made a mistake."'

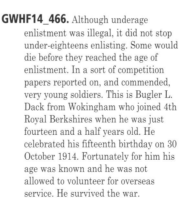

GWHF14_466. Although underage enlistment was illegal, it did not stop under-eighteens enlisting. Some would die before they reached the age of enlistment. In a sort of competition papers reported on, and commended, very young soldiers. This is Bugler L. Dack from Wokingham who joined 4th Royal Berkshires when he was just fourteen and a half years old. He celebrated his fifteenth birthday on 30 October 1914. Fortunately for him his age was known and he was not allowed to volunteer for overseas service. He survived the war.

GWHF14_467. Women also volunteered for overseas work. This is Miss C. Page-Roberts of Strathfieldsaye who was a Red Cross nurse in Belgium.

LOCAL SOLDIERS WOUNDED.

Pte. E. HAMBLING, 2nd Oxford and Bucks Infantry. 156, Cholmeley-road.

Lce.-Corpl. B. J. WILSON, 3rd Lancashire Fusiliers. 13, Great Knollys-street.

Pte. W. WARWICK, 1st Royal Berks Regt., Wokingham. (He has lost an arm.)

Lce.-Corpl. A. JARVIS, 2nd Royal Sussex Regt., 149, King's-road, Reading.

GWHF14_468. When space permitted, the papers included photos of those who had been recently wounded.

GWHF14_469. Family size was bigger at the turn of the century. Having six sons was not unusual. Again papers turned it into a competition to see which family had the most relatives with the colours. These were the sons of Mr and Mrs William Slade.

GWHF14_476. Four views of the riots in Paris.

GWHF14_492. Often something as simple as losing documents or failing to hear a challenge resulted in accusations of spying.

GWHF14_496. There were real spies. Carl Hans Lody, was tried at the Middlesex Guildhall on 30 October. He is sitting in the dock guarded by two soldiers with fixed bayonets.

GWHF14_483. Another unwelcome German and Austrian import was the spy. This purports to show a German spy caught on Montreal dock being escorted to jail.

GWHF14_502. With many Americans stranded in Britain, their government sent gold to help cover costs. Here sailors on board the USS *Tennessee* are carrying kegs of gold for the aid of US refugees.

GWHF14_503. The Santa Claus ship from the United States with big naval guns in the foreground. On 25 November, the SS *Jason* arrived at Devonport with Christmas gifts from America to the children of the belligerent countries. Aboard were 5,000,000 parcels weighing 12,000 tons in 2,000 packing cases. The next stop was Marseilles.

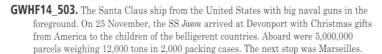

GWHF14_507. Although not officially allowed, people did not stop visiting the battlefields once the war had moved on. These are souvenir hunters at Senlis.

GWHF14_505. As in England, German children dressed in the same style as their male relatives. These three scouts are collecting gifts for the troops.

GWHF14_509. Souvenir hunters investigating an abandoned German car.

GWHF14_512. As in Britain there were appeals for men of the Jewish faith to join the army in the country's hour of need, and telling them to be prepared for any sacrifice.

An die deutschen Juden!

In schicksalsernster Stunde ruft das Vaterland seine Söhne unter die Fahnen.

Dass jeder deutsche Jude zu den Opfern an Gut und Blut bereit ist, die die Pflicht erheischt, ist selbstverständlich.

Glaubensgenossen! Wir rufen Euch auf, über das Mass der Pflicht hinaus Eure Kräfte dem Vaterlande zu widmen! Eilet freiwillig zu den Fahnen! Ihr alle — Männer und Frauen — stellet Euch durch persönliche Hilfeleistung jeder Art und durch Hergabe von Geld und Gut in den Dienst des Vaterlandes!

Berlin, den 1. August 1914.

Verband der Deutschen Juden. Centralverein deutscher Staatsbürger jüdischen Glaubens.

Section Five:
Propaganda

GWHF14_0519. Crowds in Petrograd, previously St Petersburg, celebrating the Russian victory at Lemberg.

GWHF14_0521. French field guns being displayed outside the Feldherrnhalle in Munich.

GWHF14_0522. A parade in Berlin to celebrate Sedan Day, 2 September, the anniversary of the crowning disaster for the French during the Franco-Prussian war. This success was not repeated in 1914 but the celebration went ahead to showcase French and Russian field guns captured during the German advance. The parade of captured Belgian, French and Russian guns went through the Brandenburg Gate along Pariser Platz at the end of Unter den Linden.

GWHF14_0525. Regimental flags were special prizes of war. The first captured flag of was that of the 309 French Infantry Regiment. Along with a captured machine gun, it was placed in the army museum in Munich.

GWHF14_0526. Captured Russian machine guns on display at army headquarters in Berlin.

GWHF14_0527. English field guns, captured by Saxon troops near Ypres, on display in the city square in Leipzig.

GWHF14_0530. Captured German flags being paraded before the crowds.

GWHF14_0529. Captured Russian guns on display in Vienna.

GWHF14_0536. Propaganda from the Eastern Front. A German equivalent to the British 'Are we downhearted?'

GWHF14_0549. On one side of the wire the German soldier was seen as a barbarian and violator, on the other as a friend who gave them food when they were short. The fact that they caused the shortage is of course not mentioned.

GWHF14_0550. The German soldier as the benefactor of the Belgian population.

GWHF14_0553. Six German standards captured during the Battle of the Aisne goimg on display at Les Invalides in Paris.

GWHF14_0554. The first German flag captured by the French was sent to Paris, where, before being escorted to Les Invalides, was publicly displayed in a window of the War Ministry. It was captured in Alsace and belonged to 132 Infantry regiment.

GWHF14_0555. The first German gun brought to London was captured by the 1st Lincolnshires.

GWHF14_0557. Relics of the Liège siege on display in Brussels: rifles, a helmet-cover and a Hussar's busby.

GWHF14_0556. A battle trophy in London: a Uhlan's lance-head from Haelen. The broken-off steel head of a Uhlan's lance was picked up on the field at Haelen in Belgium after the battle. Both the pennon and tip were blood stained.

GWHF14_0558. An unusual scene at the beginning of the war. By Christmas the German population were used to the arrival of hundreds of Russians at stations in the east before being marched off to their prison camp.

GWHF14_0560. A more unusual sight in Germany was a column of marching British and French officers. The officer in the centre is Colonel W. E. Gordon of the Gordon Highlanders.

GWHF14_0563. These are German POWs working in a French street.

GWHF14_0561. A sight that soon became commonplace as fewer and fewer men were available to work. Both sides used their prisoners to form working parties on the land and in the street. These are Russians, stationed at Fustenburg, who were detailed to keep the street clean.

GWHF14_0565. Prisoners often tried to escape. To prevent this, the camp at Camberley, in Surrey, had an electrified fence to keep them in and stop outsiders trading with them.

GWHF14_0570. With much of Belgium in German hands, most German captives taken in Belgium were transported to Britain. This 1,000 strong column had been captured near Aerschot and was heading for Antwerp docks. They were Landsturmm, older soldiers who, from their appearance, the original caption said, drew commiseration rather than admiration as they marched past.

GWHF14_0572. British sailors from HMS *Amphion* and German sailors from the minelayer that sunk her being buried together.

GWHF14_0573. Enemies at peace.

GWHF14_0582. Propaganda for the Home Front showing the royals doing their bit for the war effort. However, although the future King went to France he was not allowed to fight. Here he is, newly commissioned, putting his men through a course of drill at Wellington Barracks.

GWHF14_0577. 'The Brixham fishing-smack *'Provident'*, owned and skippered by William Pillar…rescued two officers and sixty-eight men of HMS *Formidable* after they had been in an open cutter for nearly twelve hours. The *'Provident'* was running to Brixham before a gale, for shelter. Off the Start, the force of the wind compelled her to heave-to after she had been struck by heavy seas. She was on the starboard tack when there was seen on the mountainous seas a small open boat flying a sailor's scarf from an oar hoisted as a staff. After a series of perilous manoeuvres, carried out with splendid seamanship, a rope was caught by the sailors in the cutter, and, eventually, the naval men were got aboard the smack.'

England Expects
Every Man . . .
To Do His Duty. . .

Trust
The Commercials.
(NORTHUMBERLAND FUSILIERS).

GWHF14_0594. In many parts of the country battalions of pals were recruited. This is a postcard telling the people in Newcastle not to worry as their 'Commercial' battalion is doing its duty.

Don't be Alarmed,
the 8th S. Wales Borderers
are on guard.

GWHF14_0595. In Wales the troops felt the same and told their families so.

FOR KING
AND
COUNTRY

"Rule Britannia,
rule the waves;
Britons never
will be slaves!"
Thomson

GWHF14_0601. And of course there was always 'Rule Britannia' to swell the ranks and make people feel more comfortable about the war.

VHF14_0608. A card that could not have been made or sold in Britain. A French use for a German helmet.

GWHF14_0615. Both sides believed that God was on their side and used religion in many different ways at home and at the front. One common theme was praying for the safe return of father.

GWHF14_0616. A German painting: faithful unto death.

GWHF14_0621. Before DORA stopped church bells ringing, many churches rang them at noon asking people to say a prayer for the soldiers and sailors. This was the sign at Eridge church.

GWHF14_0610. French alpine troops removing the border sign meant the start of the return of the lost provinces. A huge morale boost for those at home.

Section Six:
Casualties

GWHF14_624. Christ looked after the dead and the wounded. The dead looked on and it was Christ who was helping the wounded soldier not his friend.

Dem Heldentod
fürs Vaterland folgt Lohn
aus Gottes Vaterhand.

GWHF14_625. The reverse of German death card suggesting that a hero's death for the Fatherland will be rewarded in heaven.

GWHF14_633. Something that quickly became commonplace on the French Home Front: wounded being disembarked at Calais.

GWHF14_634. Many different types of ship were used to move the wounded across the Channel. This is the Great Western turbine steamer, St. Andrew, used on the Fishguard and Rosslare service. The black hull was painted white with a broad green stripe amidships intersected by the Red Cross symbol. She was scrapped in 1933.

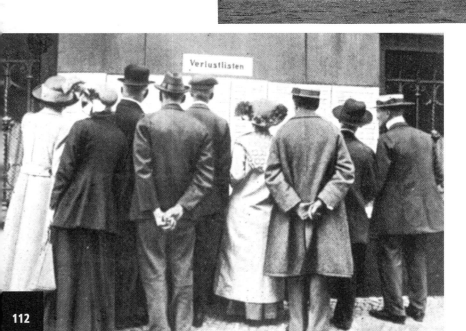

GWHF14_631. Onlookers read the latest loss list posted in a German city.

GWHF14_636. Barges were also used as efficient and cheap mass transport for the lightly wounded by the German Army. A hospital barge train heading for Berlin.

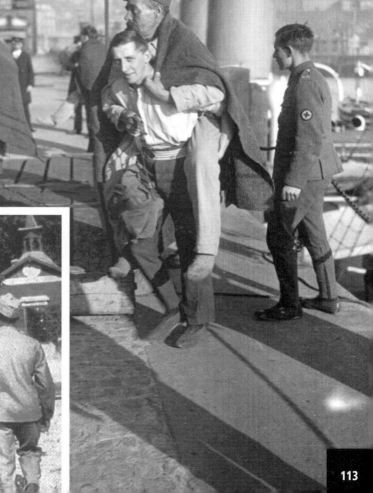

GWHF14_637. Manpower was sometimes used to bring the men ashore in England before putting them on trains that dispersed them across the nation, generally not in the direction of home.

GWHF14_638. An Austrian hospital train about to set out for field hospitals in Russia.

GWHF14_641. Ambulance trains we[re] met by military or private ambulances at mainline stations Once loaded they would drive to hospital, a war hospital or a recovery hospital.

GWHF14_642. Many organisations provided ambulances. Here the walking wounded are being met [at] Reading station. The ambulance was a converted Ford truck presented to the Royal Berkshire Regiment by the Wellington Club

GWHF14_639. A purpose-built GWR ambulance train.

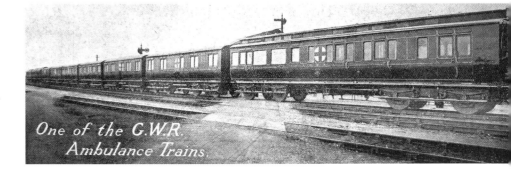

One of the G.W.R. Ambulance Trains.

GWHF14_643. A motor ambulance convoy arriving at Charing Cross hospital. The early arrivals drew large numbers of spectators but with time fewer watched such convoys.

GWHF14_646. A party of wounded soldiers reached Plymouth on 31 August and were quickly moved to Salisbury Road School. Among them were men of the Middlesex and Royal Scots Regiments which were stationed in Plymouth when the war began. By that date there were 300 men in hospital at Woolwich, 316 in the London Hospital, and 140 at Bishops Stortford. The next day 300 arrived at Brighton and about 120 each at Portsmouth and Birmingham.

GWHF14_647. Hospital barges used by the French moored in Paris after unloading their human cargo.

GWHF14_648. Brand new ambulances in the city of Posen wait for the arrival of the wounded.

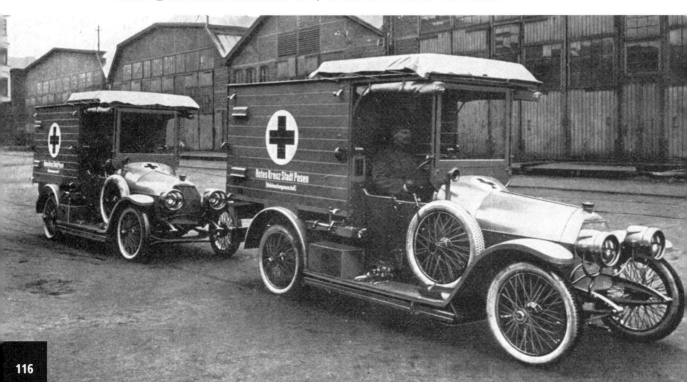

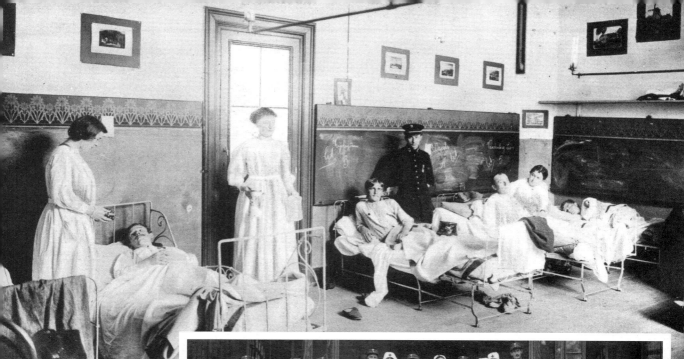

GWHF14_651. In Brussels, hotels, public institutions, schools and private dwellings were placed at the disposal of the Red Cross. This is a classroom in a Brussels school, in use as a hospital ward, where local ladies are nursing Belgian and German soldiers.

GWHF14_655. Austrian Red Cross staff and volunteers at a country house in use as a hospital.

GWHF14_649. There was not always enough space in the motor transport so bicycles were used. This is a bicycle ambulance used in Berlin. Probably not the most comfortable ride over the cobbled streets.

GWHF14_656. Volunteer male nurses in Germany.

GWHF14_657. Württemberg Red Cross volunteers being inspected by Queen Charlotte of Württemberg at a convent in use as a hospital.

GWHF14_659. Some of the wounded found themselves being nursed in places they would never normally see. Here the ballroom of the Grand Palace in Brussels is in the process of being converted into a large hospital ward.

GWHF14_658. A French department store in use as a hospital.

GWHF14_661. Raffael Hall in the Orangerieschloss (Orangery Palace of Friedrich Wilhelm IV) at Potsdam was converted in a hospital.

GWHF14_662. The converted dining room of a major Berlin restaurant finding a new use.

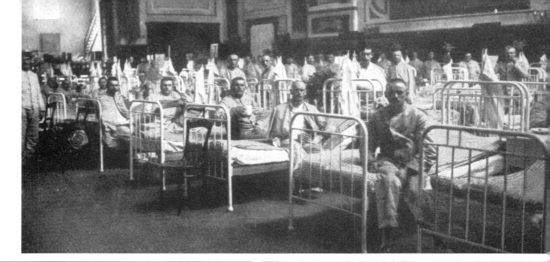

GWHF14_664. The Great Hall of Birmingham University in use as a military hospital.

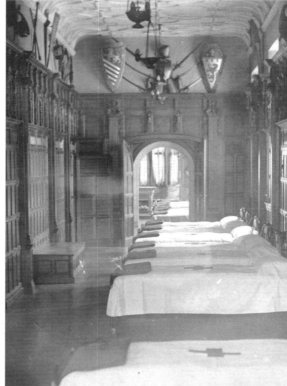

GWHF14_663. The wing of a stately home in Britain in use as a hospital.

GWHF14_671. French convalescents at a hospital at Val de Gras.

GWHF14_666. The cloisters at Trinity College, Cambridge, turned into a military hospital.

GWHF14_665. Russian aristocracy visiting the wounded in a hall in the Royal Palace in St Petersburg.

GWHF14_669. Recovering on the beach at Brighton.

GWHF14_670. German convalescents reading about their adventures in *The Illustrated History of the War*: a multi-part magazine that was produced throughout the war.

GWHF14_672. The Empress Eugenie with an officer in the grounds of her house, Farnborough Hill, part of which was a military hospital.

GWHF14_673. In Germany, Daisy, Princess of Pless, sister of the Duchess of Westminster, nursed her husband's countrymen.

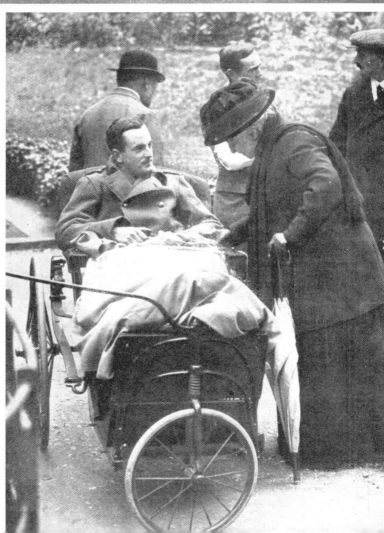

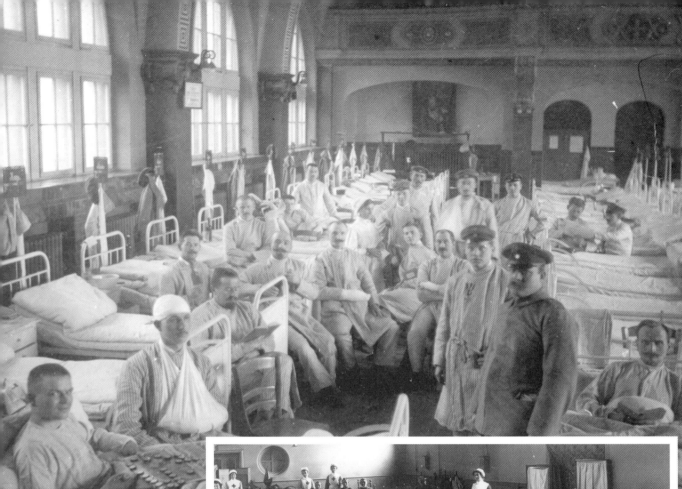

GWHF14_675. The reality of many military hospitals. This is a German hospital in Belgium.

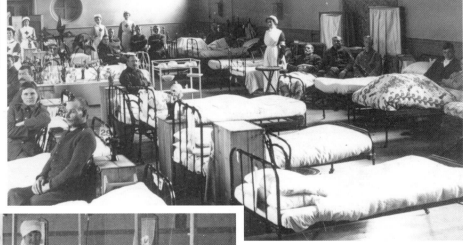

GWHF14_677. It was the same in Britain.

GWHF14_679. A corner of an Orthopaedic ward in a British hospital. It is difficult to tell the difference between the nationalities when looking at hospital ward pictures.

GWHF14_684. Some were lucky to survive their wounds. Quarter-Master Sergeant Wilkins of the 9th Lancers was still on his feet after being wounded twenty times.

GWHF14_692. Official reports were not always correct. Major Scott Turner was reported killed but was captured and wounded. The truth was only revealed when a cheque drawn in favour of the Red Cross and dated September 25th was received by his bankers.

GWHF14_689. Probably worse for those waiting at home was the news that their loved one was missing. Private Hatton was later listed as Killed in action on 26 August.

GWHF14_691. The sort of communication no one wanted. An official notification from the War Ministry that Joseph Dienst-Wiesau of 6 Landwehr Regiment was missing.

The late Pte. DANIEL ROBERTSON, Bedfordshire Regt., who died a hero's death. He faced a rain of bullets in order to fetch a wounded sergeant from the firing line and when carrying him to safety was shot down. He lived at 43, Great Knollys Street, Reading, and before the war was a taxicab driver in the town. He leaves a widow and two children.

The late Bugler FREDK. WELLS, 2nd Oxford and Bucks Light Infantry, who received five bullet wounds in the leg and died in hospital. Writing from his deathbed to his home, 107, Great Knollys Street, Reading, Wells said: "I should not have had five wounds only the Germans cowardly shot a good many of us as we lay wounded."

GWHF14_700. Neighbours serving in different regiments.

GWHF14_697. The toll on the German aristocracy was the same as in Britain. This is Prince Heinrich XLVI. Von Reuss (younger line) who was killed at La Bassée on 20 October 1914.

GWHF14_701. It was now a world war with British citizens fighting with Empire armies. Harry Street from a small village outside Reading had emigrated to Australia where he had joined the Royal Australian Navy. He was killed in action on 11 September fighting in Papua New Guinea.

GWHF14_702. Even at local level it was obvious which social echelon the deceased came from. This is Second Lieutenant E. R. Waring, 1st Battalion King's Royal Rifle Corps, who was killed in action on 28 October, six weeks short of his twenty-first birthday. Educated at Wixenford and Wellington College, he was gazetted as Second Lieutenant on 1 October 1913. The motto of the Waring family of Beenham is 'Toujours Prêt'.

HARRY STREET,
late of Earley, Reading, killed in action in the British raid on a German colony. He was an A.B. in the Royal Australian Naval Reserve, which he joined only a month before his gallant death.

GWHF14_704. A number of men died at home in accidents. This is the funeral of despatch rider Lionel Rainford who was killed on manoeuvres. Petty Officer Rainford, who died on 16 December, was buried at Larges Lane Cemetery in Bracknell with full military honours.

GWHF14_706. Overcrowding in barracks resulted in death from disease for some men, while others were killed in training. This is the funeral of a soldier from a service battalion of the Royal Berkshire Regiment.

GWHF14_710. Many families had death cards printed even though there was no funeral. It was especially common in Germany and Austria to have them printed and given to family and friends as they would have done under more normal circumstances. Private Johann Laufenböck of the 2nd Landwehr Regiment was killed in action in France on 19 August.

Christliches Andenken im Gebete
an den tugendsamen Jüngling
Johann Laufenböck
Gütler von Altötting
Soldat beim 2. Infanterie-Land-wehr-Regiment
welcher am 19. August 1914 im 29. Lebensjahre auf den Schlachtfeldern Frankreichs den Heldentod fürs Vater-land starb.

Heiligstes Herz Jesu, auf dich ver-traue ich!
[100 Tage Ablaß.]   25. Sept. 1852.

Buchdruckerei J. Lutzenberger Altötting.

Christliches Andenken
an Herrn
Johann Wollner,
**Wirtschaftsbesitzer in Schwiebgrub,
beim Inf.-Reg. 91,**

welcher zu Kriegsbeginn einrückte, am serbischen Kriegsschauplatze gekämpft hat, wo er am 15. August 1914 durch einen Kopfschuß im 34. Lebensjahre in Groß-Glava (Serbien) den Heldentod gestorben ist.

Ein schmerzlich Los, den Vater zu
verlieren,
Wer reicht den Kindern nun die
Vaterhand?
Wer wird die Kindlein leiten, wird sie
führen,
Wie es das teure Vaterherz verstand?
Doch gänzlich bist du nicht von uns
geschieden,
Nicht schließt das Grab dein ganzes
Wesen ein.
Die Seele wandert ja im ew'gen
Frieden,
Im Himmel wirst du unser Vater sein!

GWHF14_709. Austrian Johann Wollner was killed on 15 August fighting against the Serbs.

Gefallen für's Vaterland
auf dem Felde der Ehre.
Näheres nicht bekannt.
Kriegsministerium.
Zentral-Nachweise-Bureau.
Referat I.

Die Richtigkeit bescheinigt

Sekretär.

GWHF14_708. In Britain it was a telegram, in Germany it was a postcard. This postcard was sent by the German War Ministry informing the family of the death of their son.

Zur frommen Erinnerung
an den ehrengeachteten Herrn
Josef Graser,
Mesner von Kirchamper,
Reservist beim k. Infanterie-Leib-Regt.,
gestorben am 2. Oktober 1914 bei
Liben auf dem Felde der Ehre
den Heldentod fürs Vaterland im
26. Lebensjahre.

Daß Du zur Heimat wiederkehrst,
Hat nimmer sollen sein, —
Nur aus der Ferne dürfen wir
Dir heiße Tränen weihn.

Druck v. J. Pichlmayr (G.m.b.H.) Moosburg

GWHF14_712. Josef Graser was a church verger in Kirchamper before his death on 2 October near Liben. The twenty-six year-old was a reservist in the Bavarian Lifeguards Regiment.

Zum christlichen Andenken
an den ehrengeachteten
Herrn Josef Linner
Gütler von Kendling, Pfarrei
Kienberg, **Landwehrmann im**
1. Res.-Inf.-Rgt., 12. Komp.
welcher am 19. Dezember 1914 bei
St. Laurent-Arras (Nordfrankreich)
in seinem 31. Lebensjahre den
Heldentod fürs Vaterland erlitt.

Heiligstes Herz Jesu, ich vertraue
auf dich! (300 Tg. Ablaß.)
Süßester Jesus, sei mir nicht
Richter, sondern Seligmacher!
(50 Tg. Ablaß.)

Druck von Gebr. Erdl, Trostberg.

GWHF14_714. Josef Linner, Landwehrmann, fighting near Arras with a reserve infantry regiment was killed in action on 12 December.

Section Seven:
Personalities

GWHF14_715. Probably the most well-known moustache in the world at the time. Kaiser Wilhelm II ruled Germany from 1888 to 1918 when he abdicated and fled to Holland.

GWHF14_716. King Wilhelm II of Württemberg, a separate state within the German Empire ruled by the Prussian Emperor Wilhelm II.

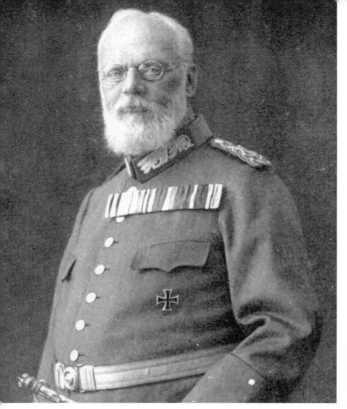

GWHF14_717. King Ludwig III of Bavaria, the second biggest state within the empire. It had its own independent armed forces.

GWHF14_718. King Friedrich August III of Saxony, a separate state on the eastern side of the empire.

GWHF14_719. Mehmed V Reshad was the 35th Ottoman Sultan; he was also the Caliph of Islam. He declared jihad against the Entente Powers on 11 November but many of his subjects took no notice and fought against the Turks to gain independence instead.

GWHF14_720. The Emperor of Austria-Hungary, Franz Joseph I, ruled his empire from 1848 to 1916.

GWHF14_721. Princess Viktoria Luise, Wilhelm's daughter, with her husband Prince Ernst August of Hannover. Their wedding was 'the largest gathering of reigning monarchs in Germany since German unification in 1871, and one of the last great social events of European royalty before World War I began fourteen months later. Attendees included Wilhelm's cousins King George V and Tsar Nicholas II, accompanied by their respective wives Queen Mary and Tsarina Alexandra. The wedding feast included 1,200 guests.'

GWHF14_722. Crown Prince Wilhelm was heir to the German Empire. 'Despite being only thirty-two and having never commanded a unit larger than a regiment he was named commander of the 5th Army in August 1914, shortly after the outbreak of World War I. His father instructed the Crown Prince to defer to the advice of his experienced Chief of Staff Schmidt von Knobelsdorf. In November 1914 Wilhelm gave his first interview to a foreign correspondent and the first statement to the press made by a German aristocrat since the outbreak of war. He said this in English: "Undoubtedly this is the most stupid, senseless and unnecessary war of modern times. It is a war not wanted by Germany, I can assure you, but it was forced on us, and the fact that we were so effectually prepared to defend ourselves is now being used as an argument to convince the world that we desired conflict."'

GWHF14_723. A German hero. Vice Admiral Maximilian Reichsgraf von Spee (22 June 1861 – 8 December 1914) was admiral in charge of Germany's East Asia Squadron. Knowing he was no match for the Allied naval forces he left China and headed for Germany through the Pacific. At the Battle of Coronel off the coast of Chile on 1 November 1914, Spee's force engaged and sank two British armoured cruisers commanded by Sir Christopher Cradock: HMS *Good Hope* and HMS *Monmouth*. Five weeks later at the Battle of the Falkland Islands, Spee's flagship, *Scharnhorst*, together with *Gneisenau*, *Nürnberg* and *Leipzig* were all lost, together with some 2,200 German sailors, including Spee himself and his two sons: his eldest son, Lt. Otto von Spee, who served aboard the *Nürnberg*, and Lt. Heinrich von Spee who served on the *Gneisenau*. The admiral went down with his flagship, the *Scharnhorst*, along with all hands.

GWHF14_724. Grand Admiral Alfred Peter Friedrich von Tirpitz (March 19, 1849 – March 6, 1930) was a German Admiral and Secretary of State of the German Imperial Naval Office. After failing to defeat the Royal Navy, he was dismissed and never regained power.

GWHF14_729. Generalleutnant Erich Friedrich Wilhelm Ludendorff (9 April 1865 – 20 December 1937) was the victor of Liège and of the Battle of Tannenberg.

GWHF14_725. Albrecht, Duke of Württemberg (23 December 1865 –
31 October 1939) was an important German military leader in
World War I and head of the Royal House of Württemberg from
1921 to his death. At the start of World War I he commanded the
German 4th Army.

GWHF14_726. Crown Prince Rupprecht of Bavaria (18 May 1869 – 2 August
1955) was the last Bavarian Crown Prince. He commanded the German
Sixth Army at the outbreak of World War I in Lorraine.

GWHF14_730. General der Infanterie Erich von Falkenhayn (11
September 1861 – 8 April 1922) was Chief of the General Staff
during the first two years of the war.

GWHF14_733. Karl Friedrich Max von Müller (June 16, 1873 – March 11,
1923) was captain of the German commerce raider, the light cruiser
SMS *Emden* which was active in the Pacific and Indian Ocean until
November, when she was defeated by HMAS *Sydney*.

GWHF14_734. Kapitänleutnant Otto Weddigen was a German national hero. On 22 September he was in command of U9 which sank the cruisers *Aboukir*, *Hogue* and *Cressy* in the English Channel.

GWHF14_740. Crown Prince Charles of Austria would become Emperor in 1916.

GWHF14_744. René Viviani, the French Pri Minister.

GWHF14_743. Raymond Poincaré, Presiden the French Republic.

Guerre Européenne

1914

GEORGE V Roi d'Angleterre

ALBERT I Roi des Belges

PIERRE I Roi de Serbie

M. R. POINCARÉ
Président de la République

NICOLAS II
Empereur de Russie

LES CHEFS D'ETAT

GWHF14_745. A French view of the relative importance of the Entente leaders.

GWHF14_747. The Czar and King George showing their close family relationship.

GWHF14_746. A French view of the importance of the Entente commanders-in-chief.

Guerre Européenne

Les Généralissimes

Général FRENCH
(Angleterre)

1914

Général JOFFRE (France)

Grand Duc NICOLAS (Russie)

GWHF14_751. Mary of Teck (Victoria Mary Augusta Louise Olga Pauline Claudine Agnes; 26 May 1867 – 24 March 1953) was Queen Consort of the United Kingdom and the British Dominions, and Empress of India, as the wife of King-Emperor George V. Although a princess of Teck, in the Kingdom of Württemberg, she was born and raised in England.

GWHF14_752. The King's eldest son, the Prince of Wales, was attached as an A.D.C to Sir John French's staff.

GWHF14_753. As the second son of the King, Prince Albert was allowed to see active service with the Royal Navy in the North Sea.

GWHF14_755. Sir Edward Grey was Foreign Minister at the time of the July crisis. At the start of the war he famously said: "The lamps are going out all over Europe; we shall not see them lit again in our lifetime."

GWHF14_754. Princess Mary appealed to the nation for funds so that every serviceman could receive a Christmas gift of a brass box with differing contents. She had initially offered to pay for it all herself but this was not allowed, so the British Public paid instead.

GWHF14_756. Herbert Asquith, Prime Minister of Britain from 1908 to 1916, when he was replaced by Lloyd George.

GWHF14_757. Lords Haldane (left) and Kitchener at the War Office. Lord Kitchener had been appointed Minister of War in succession to the Prime Minister on 6 August. Haldane had held the position from 1905 to 1912.

GWHF14_758. Lloyd George was Chancellor of the Exchequer at the start of the war. He would become Prime Minister in 1916.

GWHF14_760. Security, in Belgium, even in wartime, was very relaxed. The King of Belgium's two sons on walk-about in Brussels.

GWHF14_762. Field Marshal Sir John French was appointed to command the British Expeditionary Force.

GWHF14_765. The First Sea Lord, H.S.H. Prince Louis of Battenburg, a naturalised British subject, resigned from his position because it was felt his origins - he was born in Austria - might affect his judgement.

GWHF14_766. Lord Fisher, although over seventy, returned to the position of First Sea Lord when Prince Louis resigned.

GWHF14_768. Although eighty-two years-old, Field Marshal Earl Roberts went to France to visit the troops. He caught a chill and passed away peacefully on 14 November on active service.

GWHF14_767. Admiral of the Fleet Sir John Rushworth Jellicoe, GCB OM GCVO SGM (5 December 1859 – 20 November 1935), was a Royal Navy officer. He fought in the Egyptian war and in the Boxer Rebellion, and would command the Grand Fleet at the Battle of Jutland in May 1916.

GWHF14_769. Lord Roberts' coffin arriving at St. Paul's on 19 November. 'The coffin, draped with the Union Jack and bearing on top his service cap, medals, and Field Marshal's baton, was drawn from Charing Cross to the Cathedral on a gun-carriage of "P" Battery of the Royal Horse Artillery.'

GWHF14_770. After the funeral the coffin was placed in the grave and guarded by four sergeants of the Irish Guards while the public filed past to pay their respects.

Section Eight:
Refugees

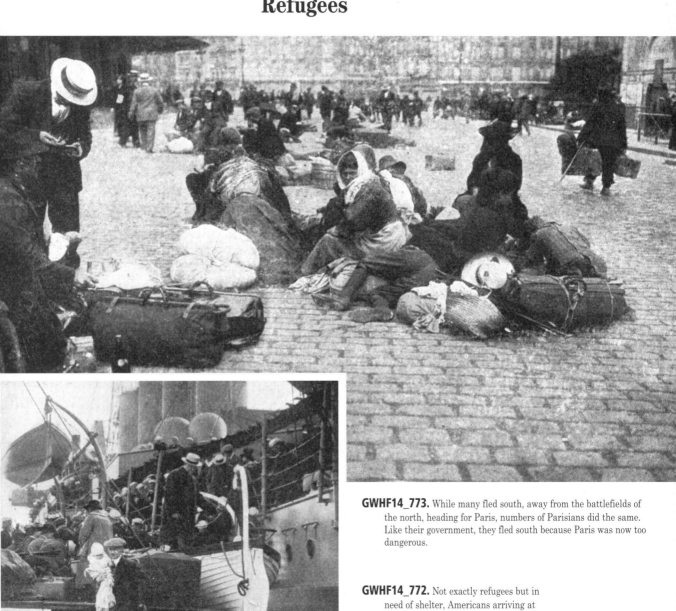

GWHF14_773. While many fled south, away from the battlefields of the north, heading for Paris, numbers of Parisians did the same. Like their government, they fled south because Paris was now too dangerous.

GWHF14_772. Not exactly refugees but in need of shelter, Americans arriving at Weymouth, from France, aboard the American cruiser, USS *Tennessee*, that had brought gold to Britain.

GWHF14_774. There were so many refugees that any space was deemed suitable. These are offices at the Gare du Nord.

GWHF14_776. The commander of the German Volunteer Automobile Corps is trying to keep traffic flowing smoothly through Lille.

GWHF14_777. Belgian refugees also headed to Paris. This group arrived in comparative comfort.

GWHF14_778. It was the same on the Eastern Front. These are Austrian refugees who have fled from the advancing Russians and arrived safely in Vienna, well behind the lines.

GWHF14_780. Many East Prussians reached Berlin where they were accommodated in disused barracks.

GWHF14_782. The refugee camp set up on FroebelStrasse in Berlin.

Saal 6.

GWHF14_784. East Prussian refugees lint plucking while at school in Berlin.

GWHF14_785. A home in Berlin for refugee girls.

GWHF14_786. There was little for the refugees to do initially except wander around the camp and talk.

GWHF14_787. For obvious reasons, smoking was not allowed in the sleeping rooms.

GWHF14_790. East Prussian farmers returning home after the Russians had retreated.

GWHF14_791. Safety but nowhere to go. East Prussians arrive in a city so far unaffected by the war. Note that the children have no footwear.

GWHF14_792. A street in an East Prussian town after a Russian bombardment.

GWHF14_793. Refugees from France and Alsace gathering at the Red Cross headquarters at Singen in Baden near the Swiss border.

GWHF14_794. The biggest exodus was from Belgium, many of whose nationals landed in Britain. This is a group of families at a large private house, Sutherlands, in Reading.

GWHF14_796. In the confusion of the German bombardment, many Belgian refugee families were separated. At the Dutch frontier town of Rosenthal, they wrote messages in chalk, stating their destination, hoping that friends and relatives would find them. The Dutch treated them with kindness and many took them into their homes.

GWHF14_797. A farmer's wife leading their horse and cart to safety. Her husband had been called up to fight leaving her in charge of the farm.

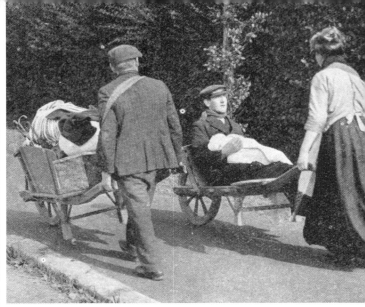

GWHF14_802. 'Before Brussels fell, thousands of terror-stricken Belgian peasants crowded into the capital from outlying districts.' As the Germans moved closer the refugees moved on. Here a wife is wheeling her sick husband, who holds their baby, in a barrow along the road to Antwerp.

GWHF14_801. 'Frightened out of Brussels by the arrival of the German Army', this crippled woman 'was wheeled to Ghent in a barrow, carrying all the worldly possessions she was able to collect hastily.'

GWHF14_803. Refugees from Antwerp crowding the quays at Ostend waiting for a boat to England.

GWHF14_807. A Young Belgian looks after her family's belongings during the long wait to leave by boat.

VHF14_805. Two refugees separated from their families wait at the quayside to escape to England.

GWHF14_804. The numbers trying to escape ran into the thousands.

GWHF14_808. Not everyone was allowed to leave. This photo was taken at Malines station where German troops were placed to stop people leaving.

GWHF14_810. A number of wounded Belgians were treated in England and many thanked their carers with a photo.

Section Nine:
News

GWHF14_812. The first official cards to arrive in homes across the country were Field Service postcards which the sender had to pay for. There was a series of sentences on the reverse for the soldier to add to or delete; a standard format that did not change. Anything else added meant the card might not get through. The postal charge was soon removed and mail from soldiers was sent free.

GWHF14_814. Many regiments and charities raised money for goods to be sent to soldiers. In return individual subscribers would receive a postcard from the recipient. This is a thank you for tobacco and cigarettes.

GWHF14_816. Field postcards were used by all the combatant armies. Those of the German Army were blank on the reverse for a personal message rather the few limited sentences provided on a British card. Many German cards were illustrated on the address side and gave detailed information about the sender.

GWHF14_817. Some were patriotic, others militaristic.

GWHF14_818. Product placement is not a new idea. This field postcard was sponsored by Alpha, a dairy company which also had offices in Britain.

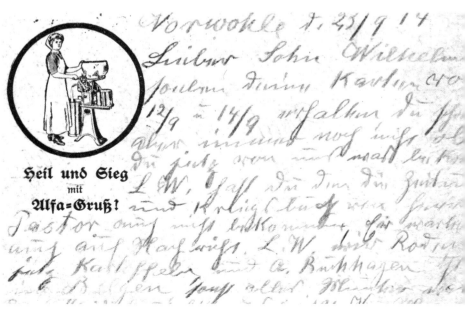

GWHF14_820. Initially French cards were simple blank cards but like their German counterparts, they soon became more decorative; usually with Allied flags.

GWHF14_821. Another new type of correspondence card was from POWs. This is from a French captive in Germany.

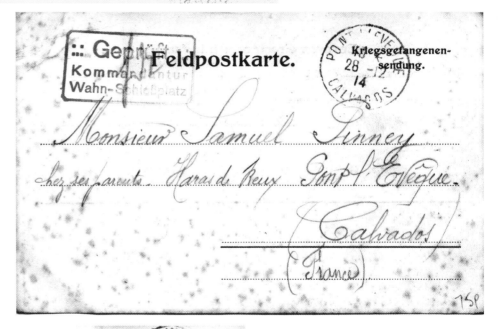

GWHF14_822. This is an interesting internal card from an English prisoner with a German surname to the branch of his family that had stayed in Germany as German citizens.

GWHF14_874. Clearing mines was potentially lethal work. This is HMT *Passing 58*, a Fleetwood trawler sailing out of Grimsby, that struck a mine while clearing the newly German-laid Scarborough minefield. Although severely holed she did not sink and was towed into Scarborough harbour by the paddle steamer Brighton Queen. It was claimed the hole was big enough to drive a horse and cart through. Her skipper George W. Thornton was commended for 'good service done under dangerous conditions.'

WITH THE SAUCY ' ARETHUSA.'

An interesting letter has been received by Mrs. Barnes, of 5, Harbert Cottages, Littlewick Green, from her son, Seaman Henry Boulter, who is serving on H.M.S. "Arethusa," which took such a prominent part in the naval battle off Heligoland. "We have had a bit of a brush with the Germans and I suppose you have seen by the papers that we had the best of it. We lost 12 poor chaps and 14 more got injured. It was a go in, I can tell you. We were in action for over six hours, and I can tell you ' we didn't half get our own back.' All our jolly lads were thirsting for a battle, and they let themselves go. I expect we shall be laid up for some time as our ship got damaged a bit, but we hope to be out by the time the next one comes off. I don't think they will be caught napping like that again."

GWHF14_864. Although censorship was supposed to be strict, as long as a letter contained no details of army units or place, the contents could be very graphic. The sailor who wrote this does not mention his ship; that information came from his mother.

HAVOC OF SEA BATTLE.

A grim account of the naval battle off Heligoland is given by Reggie White, of Bath-road, Thatcham, a seaman on board H.M.S. Archer. "I cannot describe what it looks like to see the flames coming out of the guns, men in the water, ships on fire, and the worst—no land in sight. The nearest is Germany, 26 miles away, and I should not care to go there. When it was over we went aboard the cruisers as they were sinking, and the sight was too terrible to describe—blood everywhere. Our guns were red-hot afterwards. Shot and shell were flying all around us, and this was not very comfortable.'

GWHF14_867. A graphic letter about the Heligoland Blight battle.

GWHF14_872. The British coast was defended by fixed minefields which could be safely navigated but German ships and submarines laid mines in supposedly safe areas. They were sometimes washed ashore after rough weather. This was washed up on the East Coast in October and landed upside down on the beach.

GWHF14_876. Whitby lifeboat men attempting to launch their boat.

GWHF14_875. Not all ships were lost to enemy action. HMHS *Rohilla* was a passenger steamer converted into a hospital ship. On 30 October she ran aground on Saltwick Nab, a reef about a mile east of Whitby during a full south-westerly gale. Five lifeboats attempted to close on the wreck. Out of a crew of 229, 146 survived, including the captain, all the nurses and a *Titanic* survivor, Mary Roberts.

GWHF14_877. A survivor is helped ashore. Some had taken refuge in what was left of the centre of the hull and managed to swim ashore over the next three days. Many did not survive the swim.

GWHF14_879. Heavy losses at sea increased the number of orphans. Twenty new arrivals at Newland Orphan Home in Hull. They were the children of men who had lost their lives on HMS *Cressy*, *Aboukir* and *Hogue* or on minesweepers.

GWHF14_881. In Germany the men of *U9* were feted as heroes and awarded the Iron Cross for their part in the sinking of three British cruisers.

GWHF14_878. Another ship lost, again not to enemy forces, was HMS *Bulwark*. 'On 26 November 1914, while anchored near Sheerness, she was destroyed by a large internal explosion for the loss of 736 men. Two of the 14 survivors died later in hospital. The explosion was likely to have been caused by the overheating of cordite charges that had been placed adjacent to a boiler room bulkhead.'

Section Ten:
Raids and occupation

GWHF14_882. Baby-killers to the Allies, but heroic defenders to the German people. The Zeppelin shed at Düsseldorf was the first place in Germany to be bombed. The German Home Front in the west became a potential war zone on 23 September.

GWHF14_884. Searchlights were quickly set up to discourage night time intruders and allow gunners to see them. This is the searchlight at Charing Cross station.

GWHF14_885. Paris by night. A searchlight shines above the Place de la Concorde.

GWHF14_886. In Rheims, the cellars became shelters where people lived.

GWHF14_889. A large crowd is gathering to watch a German Taube aircraft fly over Paris.

GWHF14_892. The ruined city of Lille. This is the corner of Marché aux Poulets and Rue Faidherbe after the German bombardment. Life continued as close to normal as possible when the streets were cleared.

GWHF14_890. Damage in the Rue Vinaigriers caused by bombs dropped from about 7,000 feet on 30 August. Two women were wounded and many windows smashed.

GWHF14_893. Lille the day after it was captured. Even with dead horses on the street there are still people walking about.

GWHF14_902. Numbers 20 and 21 Cleveland Street, West Hartlepool.

GWHF14_904. Three people were killed in the house on the left in Lily Street, West Hartlepool.

GWHF14_909. The barracks in the grounds of Scarborough Castle.

GWHF14_905. The first shell hit the cliff giving time to evacuate the signal-station. The second shell smashed into the station and partially demolished it. Frederick Randall, a coastguard, was killed by one of the shells.

GWHF14_910. The only artillery piece in Scarborough was this old cannon.

GWHF14_911. Business as usual at Merryweather's food store. His wife was killed during the bombardment as she took some ladies down to the cellar for safety.

GWHF14_912. 'The harbour-master, who was looking in the direction at the moment, saw the projectile strike and then glance off, landing in the Grand Hotel, which suffered from a number of German shells during the bombardment.'

GWHF14_913. Four people were killed at 2 Wykeham Street.

GWHF14_915. A number of people were injured by the shelling. This is the women's ward in Scarborough hospital where casualties were treated.

GWHF14_917. In times like this, much reliance was placed upon volunteer assistance. The Red Cross held more flag days than any other organisation during the war.

GWHF14_918. In Paris, the residents were bombed and, as the Germans drew closer to the city, plans were made to defend it. Parisians expected a siege. A queue to buy provisions before the worst happened.

GWHF14_919. A quartet of photos showing how Paris prepared for the envisaged German siege of the city.

GWHF14_920. On 1 September, the Military Governor of Paris gave final directions for the precautionary measures to be taken against a siege of the capital. Cattle and fodder were called in from the surrounding country and placed in convenient open spaces round the city. All the cattle were collected together at the Longchamps race-course to the west of the city, famous in pre-war days for the Grand Prix.

GWHF14_921. Paris under the threat of another Prussian siege. A scene in Rue Faubourg St. Antoine, where a horse had just been killed by a bomb dropped in front of the Hospital St. Antoine.

GWHF14_922. Parisians building a barricade to defend the city.

GWHF14_925. The new Belgian government was all German.

GWHF14_926. Cities, towns and villages had to get used to Germans marching through. A naval parade through Antwerp.

GWHF14_927. For the people of Amiens, it was a short occupation. The Germans captured the city on 31 August but were evicted by the French two weeks later.

GWHF14_928. Those unable to provide for themselves had to rely on their occupier to feed them. A propaganda photo to show the generosity of the German troops.

GWHF14_932. German troops giving out a coal ration to the occupants of Lodz.

GWHF14_929. As on the Western Front, civilians in the east had to get used to enemy troops occupying their town or village. Here Russians are marching through a newly captured town.

GWHF14_931. Russian women being questioned in the street.

Section Eleven:
Joining in

GWHF14_934. A well-known speaker would always draw a big crowd. There were no spare seats when Lord Curzon spoke about the war on 14 September.

GWHF14_935. The audience at the Guildhall on 4 September to hear Mr Asquith justify Britain's entrance into the Great War. He appealed to the patriotism of the citizens of London, emphasizing the efforts made to preserve peace and paying tribute to the splendid response of the British Empire to the call to arms.

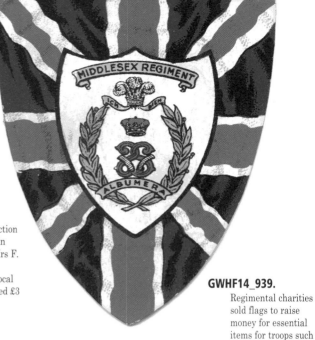

GWHF14_937. Another method was the collection box carried by those in need of the money. Mrs F. J. Lewis took some Belgian boys to two local army camps and raised £3 5s.

GWHF14_939. Regimental charities sold flags to raise money for essential items for troops such as tobacco.

GWHF14_941. Before the practice was stopped, very young children willingly gave their time to help raise money. This boy was raising funds for the Red Cross.

GWHF14_942. Two girls collecting for the Red Cross.

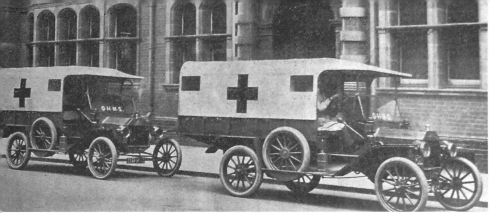

GWHF14_943. Two ambulances touring Reading during a Red Cross collection day.

GWHF14_944. Animals were used to raise money for animal charities like the Blue Cross for horses.

GWHF14_949. The very rich often lent or bought things rather than giving money. This convoy of 60 ambulances, wagons and motor-cycles was a Christmas gift for the British Army from Maharaja Scindia of Gwalior.

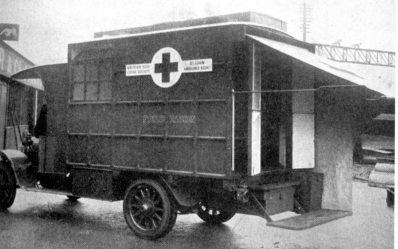

GWHF14_950. Lord Tredegar loaned his luxury yacht *Liberty* and paid for it to be converted into a hospital ship. He offered to continue paying all the expenses for the duration, and in return was commissioned in the RNR as a Lieutenant and allowed to command the ship.

GWHF14_951. This mobile field kitchen was presented to the Red Cross by the Worshipful Company of Leathersellers.

GWHF14_952. German schoolgirls making bandages for the war hospitals.

GWHF14_953. Society women sewing woollen shirts for soldiers aboard Lord Tredegar's hospital yacht: a Red Cross sewing meeting in Claridge's Hotel.

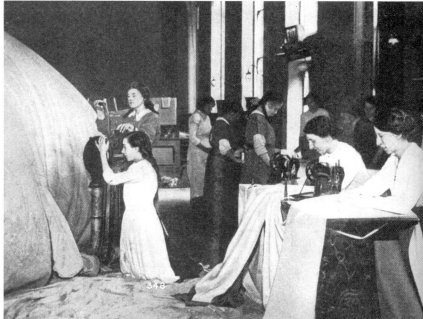

GWHF14_954. Women working in a balloon factory where their seamstress skills proved very useful.

GWHF14_958. Many of the older men joined quasi-military organisations to help their country. This is a German Red Cross officer.

GWHF14_960. Some joined the men's branch of the VAD and wore only the armband and unit badge until sufficient uniforms were available. This man was a member of the 1st Devon VAD based in Exeter.

GWHF14_961. Others joined the special constabulary. This is a member of the Essex 'specials'.

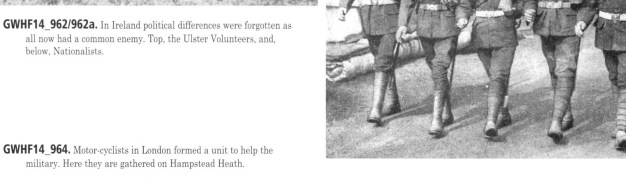

GWHF14_962/962a. In Ireland political differences were forgotten as all now had a common enemy. Top, the Ulster Volunteers, and, below, Nationalists.

GWHF14_964. Motor-cyclists in London formed a unit to help the military. Here they are gathered on Hampstead Heath.

GWHF14_965. Those too young, like these Eton schoolboys, learned how to march and drill. Most would join as officers when they were old enough.

GWHF14_966. One of the first women's organisations to be set up was the Women's Volunteer Reserve. It pledged to assist the government and country in any possible way.

GWHF14_967. Many helped in any way they could. Here a London chef is teaching scouts how to cook for large numbers.

GWHF14_969. Women quickly took over many jobs, especially in the munitions factories. This is Leeds Ammunition Factory where the women are making cartridge cases.

GWHF14_970. In France, women quickly replaced men in traditionally male employment. A female tramcar operative.

GWHF14_972. These schoolboys in their workshop in Ponders End in Middlesex are learning how to make munitions as part of their general education.

GWHF14_978. Displaced families, when resettled in cities like Berlin, needed household goods. In Germany there were furniture collections to solve the problem.

GWHF14_977. Munitions work was speeded up where possible. This was easy to achieve for small scale items but large gun manufacture took time and skilled labour. This is the Krupp plant in Essen.

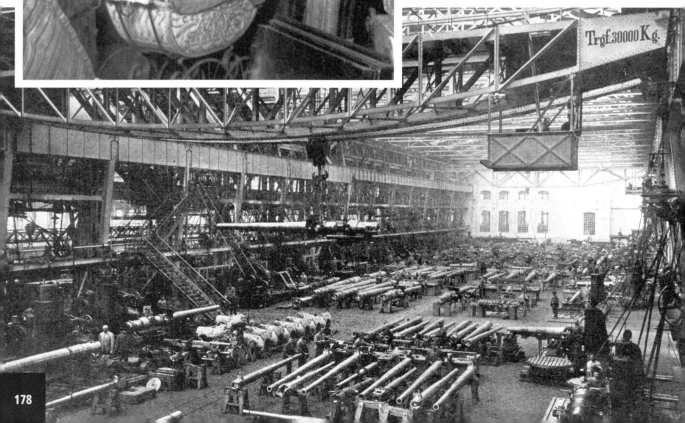

Section Twelve:
Christmas

GWHF14_995. Every effort was made to keep the season special for the children. Here Santa visits a school to give out gifts.

GWHF14_993. One Christmas gift needed in the trenches was a Christmas pudding. This is part of a shipment sent from a manufacturer in Berkshire.

GWHF14_996. The soldiers in the trenches received so many presents that the postal system couldn't always cope. This is the central sorting office in Berlin for army mail.

GWHF14_999. Soldiers of the Royal Berkshire Regiment enjoying their Christmas meal.

GWHF14_997. Boxloads of presents for German troops from the German Mothers' Organisation.

HERZLICHEN GRUSS

WEIHNACHTEN
1914.

fröhliche Weihnachten 1914-15
für die Soldaten im felde.

GWHF14_1003. The traditional Christmas tree is being used here to emphasise the need for Red Cross funding through charity cards.

GWHF14_1004. Christmas graffiti on a wall somewhere in Germany.

GWHF14_1006. A card from a German soldier to his family emphasising the different Christmas they will all have.

EINEN HERZLICHEN
WEIHNACHTSGRUSS!

Best · Wishes · for ·
Freedom · Happiness
and Prosperity

GWHF14_1007. In Britain many cards were patriotic as well. Kitchener above a standard Christmas wish with a difference.

GWHF14_1014. On the Japanese Home Front little was different now the Pacific had been cleared of the enemy, except for the POWs they had captured in China. Here, some of these are under guard.

The Boys behind the Maxim Gun
Wish all at home the best of fun,
A Happy Christmas, and Good Cheer
We'll soon be home, so never fear.

—F.E.S.

From

MACHINE GUN SECTION,
LONDON RIFLE BRIGADE,
BRITISH EXPEDITIONARY FORCE

Christmas, 1914.

GWHF14_1009. A more unusual Christmas card was sent by members of the London Rifle Brigade machine gun section their families in London.

GWHF14_1010. A deeply patriotic Christmas card.

For God,
King and
the dear
Homeland.

The Season's Greetings

Day by day chronology

August

1   British ships detained in German ports. Belgium, Denmark, Holland, Norway and Switzerland mobilise. Germany under 'Law of Siege'.

2   The Government assures France that the British Fleet will stop the German Fleet if they attack French shipping in the Channel. German unions and employers agree to a truce for the duration. France declares 'State of Siege' putting railways and country under military control. Britain mobilises remaining RN and medical reserves. One month postponement on bills of exchange, other than cheques, announced.

3   The King of the Belgians appeals to King George V for diplomatic intervention to safeguard Belgian integrity. In Trafalgar Square, Keir Hardie and George Lansbury speak out against the war. Britain orders a general mobilisation. Germany declares war on France.

4   Germany declares war on Belgium. Sweden mobilises. Sir Edward Grey wires to Sir E Goschen telling him that unless satisfactory German assurances regarding Belgian neutrality are forthcoming, he will ask for his passport. British mobilisation orders issued. Sir John Jellicoe takes control of the British Fleet. British ultimatum to Germany ends with a state of war at 11pm.

5   Austria declares war on Russia and Montenegro declares war on Austria. MI5 arrest twenty-one German spies and 200 suspects. Irish Nationalists back the war. Lord Kitchener becomes Secretary of State for War.

6   Serbia declares war on Germany. French Prime Minister appeals to women to bring in the harvest. Parliament votes £100 million for the war. Prime Minister Asquith speaks in the Commons on the war. Postal Orders become legal tender. Prince of Wales National Relief Fund opened.

7   British banks re-open and issue 10 shilling notes. German banks in Britain closed.

8   Defence of the Realm Act (DORA) passed. Appeal for 100,000 men to join the army.

9   Austria declares war on Montenegro.

10 Aliens Restriction (No. 2) Order stopped enemy aliens engaging in any banking business without written permission from the Home Secretary. France declares war on Austria. Kaiser swears to Prussian Guard leaving Berlin that he will not sheathe his sword until peace can be dictated.

11 Press Bureau constituted. 'Business as usual' motto first appears in *The Daily Chronicle*.

12 Great Britain declares war on Austria-Hungary.

13 Mrs Pankhurst suspends WSPU activities.

14 Belgium rations bread. In France rents frozen. H.G. Wells calls the conflict 'The War to end War.'

15 Bertrand Russell protests against the war in *The Nation*. Germany calls up the Landsturm.

17 Enrolment of Special Constables begins. Flour prices fixed. Soup kitchens open in Paris, serving 6,000 meals a day.

18

19 French miners' working day extended to eleven hours. 150 civilians shot at Aerschot in Belgium.

20 Queen's Work for Women Fund launched. Postal censorship starts. 311 civilians shot at Andenne.

22 Austria declares war on Belgium. Liquor sales prohibited for the duration in Russia. 384 civilians shot in Tamines.

23 612 Dinant residents massacred. Japan declares war on Germany.

24 TUC-Labour industrial truce declared.

25 Japan declares 'State of War' with Austria.

28 Appeal for a further 100,000 men for the army.

31 Unemployment 22.4% in Germany and 43% in France.

September

2 French government leaves Paris for Bordeaux. In Berlin captured guns paraded.

3 Paris Bourse closes. Queen Mary starts Work for Women Fund.

4 The Prime Minister in a speech at the Guildhall justifies Britain's entry into the war. London pub closing hour 11pm instead of 12.30.

5 Agreement of London – Great Britain, France and Russia pledge not to make a separate peace. First 'Your King and Country Need You' posters.

6 Formation of a Royal Naval Division announced by the Admiralty. Tilbury-Antwerp refugee boat service begins.

8 Speech by Lloyd George on the need for economy. Christabel Pankhurst tells London suffragettes that women should be used to the full.

14 King and Queen visit wounded officers at Princess Henry of Battenberg's Hospital in London.

18 Trading with the Enemy Act passed imposing severe penalties by way of fine and imprisonment upon any person trading with the enemy.

19 Lloyd George makes a speech to Welsh men about German barbarities.Home Secretary grants licences to allow certain German and Austrian banks to continue operating in the United Kingdom.

25 The Prime Minister, in a speech in Dublin, appeals to volunteers.

26 King, Queen and Kitchener inspect 140,000 recruits at Aldershot.
28 Prince Louis of Battenburg resigns as First Sea Lord.
29 Lord Fisher appointed as First Sea Lord.

October
1 War bread (K brot) with ersatz content introduced in Germany. 2 The German spy, Carl Lody, is arrested.
8 Proclamation allowing licenses for trading with the enemy.
12 Trial of Gavrilo Princip and associates for high treason starts in Sarajevo.
14 Certain German and Austrian banks granted licenses to receive dividends on certain shares. First Canadian troops land at Plymouth.
24 Importation of sugar prohibited. In France Teachers' Federation Journal is suspended for opposing the war.
29 Turkey enters the war on the German side. National Union of Women
Workers' Police Patrols officially set up by the Home Office.
30 Trial of Karl Lody begins.

November
1 956 schools in use by the military.
4 King, Queen and Kitchener inspect Canadian Expeditionary Force.
5 Great Britain declares war on Turkey and annexes Cyprus. Zanzibar also declares war on Turkey. The Kaiser is removed from the Navy List of officers.
6 Carl Hans Lody is the first German spy to be shot, executed by firing squad in the Tower of London.
9 Prime Minister gives a speech at the London Guildhall setting out the war aims of the Allies: "We shall never sheathe the sword".
11 Parliament opens.
14 Field Marshal Roberts dies in France.
16 Asquith moves war credit of £225 million. 14,500 enemy aliens interned in Britain.
17 £350 million war loan issue. Lloyd George's first war budget.
20 Drink sales to women prohibited before 11.30 am. Belgian Flag Day in France.
27 Trading with the Enemy Act amended to create custodians of enemy property in Great Britain.
28 Everyone checking into a hotel must register with the police.
30 King leaves England on a visit to the army in France. Rodin presents twenty works of art to the V&A museum as a thank you to the BEF. The Home Secretary grants licenses for certain Turkish banks to continue trading.

December

1   Retail food price index up by 16% since start of war.

2   Seditious paper seized in Dublin.

5   1,000 German PoWs land at Southend.

6   Pope tries to bring about a Christmas truce.

7   Paris Bourse reopens. Compulsory registration of Belgian citizens in Britain.

8   Trial of Ahlers for high treason starts.

9   Ahlers convicted, sentenced to death.

15   1915 class called-up in France.

16   Scarborough, Whitby and Hartlepool bombarded by the German navy – 137 killed and 592 injured.

17   Coastal property war insurance rates raised after German naval raids.

18   Conviction of Ahlers quashed.

21   First German air raid – seaplane from Zeebrugge drops two bombs in Dover harbour, another drops bomb near the castle. No casualties.

22   War now costing Britain £14.5 million per week.

25   Seaplane raider flies up Thames estuary – no casualties.

28   Londoners warned to use basements in case of an air attack.

31   In Russia prices have risen overall by 40% since August.

Bibliography, Sources and Further Reading

Baer, C. H. *Der Völkerkreig*. Volume 1 and 2. Julius Hoffmann. 1916
British Food Policy during the First World War. Allen & Unwin. 1985.
Becker, J. *The Great War and the French People*. Berg. 1990.
Bilton, D. *Hull in the Great War*. Pen & Sword. 2015.
Bilton, D. *Reading in the Great War*. Pen & Sword. 2015.
Bilton, D. *The Home Front in the Great War – Aspects of Conflict*. Leo Cooper. 2003.
Charman, I. *The Great War, The People's Story*. Random House. 2014.
Chickering, R. *Imperial Germany and the Great War, 1914-1918*. Cambridge University Press. 2005.
Fridenson, P. (Ed.) *The French Home Front 1914-1918*. Berg. 1992.
Gregory, A. *The Last Great War. British Society and the First World War.* Cambridge University Press. 2008.
Hastings, M. *Catastrophe*. William Collins. 2013.
Herwig, H.H. *The First World War. Germany and Austria-Hungary 1914-1918*. Arnold. 1997.
Horn, P. *Rural Life in England in the First World War*. Gill and MacMillan. 1984.
Kennedy, R. *The Children's War*. Palgrave Macmillan. 2014.
Kocka, J. *Facing Total War. German Society 1914-1918*. Berg. 1984.
Markham, J. *Keep the Home Fires Burning*. Highgate Publications. 1988
Martin, C. *English Life in the First World War*. Wayland. 1974.
Marwick, A. *The Deluge. British Society and the First World War*. Macmillan. 1973.
Marwick, A. *Women at War*. Fontana. 1977.
Reetz, W. *Eine ganze Welt gegen uns*. Ullstein. 1934.
Rex, H. *Der Weltkrieg in seiner rauhen wirklichkeit*. Hermann Rutz. 1926.
Stein, W. *Um Vaterland und Freiheit* Volumes 1 and 2. Hermann Montanus. 1915.
The Berkshire Chronicle.
The Eastern Daily News.
The Hull Times.
The Hull Daily Mail.
The Reading Mercury.
The Reading Observer.
The Reading Standard.
Turner, E.S. *Dear Old Blighty*. Michael Joseph. 1980.
Various. *Thuringen im und nach dem Weltkrieg*. Lippold. 1920.
Williams, J. *The Home Fronts*. Constable & Co Ltd. 1972.
Winter, J. M. *The Experience of World War 1*. Equinox (Oxford) Ltd. 1986.

Winter, J. *The First World War*. Volume III Civil Society. Cambridge University Press. 2014.

Wilson, H.W. (Ed.) *The Great War. The Standard History of the All Europe Conflict*. Volumes 1, 2 and 3. Amalgamated Press 1914 and 1915.

Periodicals

Die Woche, *issues 40, 45 and 50. August Scherl. 1914.*

Großer Bilder Atlas des Weltkrieges. *Volumes 1, 2, 3, 4 & 5. Bruckemann. 1915.*

History of the War. *Volumes 1, 2,3 and 4. The Times. 1914 and 1915.*

The Illustrated War News. *Volumes 1, 2, 3 and 4. Illustrated London News and Sketch, Ltd., 1914 & 1915.*

Illustrated London News. *July – December 1914. Illustrated London News and Sketch Ltd., 1914.*

Illustrierte Geschichte des Weltkrieges 14/19 *Volume 1 and 2. Union Deutsche Verlagsgesellschaft. 1919.*

Kreigsalbum. Sonderheft der Woche *No. 22 and 23. August Scherl. 1914.*

Kreigsausgabe Zeit in Bild. *Paß and Garleb. 1914.*

Kriegschronik August 1914 – Juli 1915. *1915.*

Punch, *Volume CXLVII. Punch. 1914.*

Kamerad in Westen. *Societäts-verlag/Frankfurt am Main. 1930.*

Index

Alsace, 21, 36, 103, 146

Aldershot, 55, 185

Aliens, 11, 12, 39, 183, 185

America/United States, 41, 73, 96, 141

Asquith, 83, 137, 169, 183–5

Australia, 67, 69, 125

Austria, 9, 11, 18, 27, 37, 53–4, 57, 62, 64, 96, 113, 117, 126–7, 130, 134, 138, 143, 183–5

Austrian Army, 18, 27–8, 37, 53–4, 57, 63–4, 101, 127

BEF, 41, 185

Belgium/Belgians, 8, 10, 79, 93, 100, 102, 104, 106, 117, 123, 138, 142, 147–50, 166, 170, 183–6

Berkshire, 20, 39, 88, 93, 114, 126, 179–80

Berlin, 9–13, 16, 27, 32–3, 53, 58, 82, 85, 90–1, 100, 113, 117, 119–20, 143–4, 178, 180, 183–4

Birmingham, 11, 115, 120

Bombs/Bombing/Bombardment, 14, 146–7, 157, 159, 162–3, 165, 186

Books, 90

Bracknell, 126

Bread, 13, 184–5

Britain/British, 7, 9–14, 16–17, 19–20, 23, 34–5, 40, 47, 65, 72–3, 75, 78, 80–1, 96, 98, 102, 105–106, 109, 120, 123, 125, 127, 132, 136–8, 141, 147, 152, 154, 156, 169, 171, 182–6

British Army, 35, 37–9, 42, 55, 60–1, 64–72, 74–81, 86–7, 93–6, 107, 113, 124–6, 151, 171, 180

Buckingham Palace, 10, 34, 64, 68

Caillaux, Henriette, 20

Canada/Canadians, 41, 56, 68–70, 72, 185

Casualties, 79, 111, 163, 186

Censorship, 14, 151, 184

Christmas, 14, 96, 104, 137, 171, 179–82, 186

Civilian, 7–8, 10–14, 28, 38, 44, 63, 82, 168, 184

Coal/coalminers, 168

Conscription, 7

Cyprus, 185

Death, 93, 109, 111, 126–8, 133, 159, 186

Declaration of war, 11, 31–5, 37

Defence of the Realm Act (DORA), 12, 14, 110, 183

Dover, 186

Drink, 185

Drunkenness, 72

Dublin, 184, 186

Duke Albrecht of Württemberg, 133

Emperor Franz-Joseph, 130

Entente, 130, 135

Essex, 65, 174

Eton, 176

Falkenhayn, Erich von, 133

Flag(s), 9, 34, 54, 100–101, 103, 153, 170

Flag days, 14, 163, 170, 185

Flagship(s), 10, 132

Flour, 10, 184

Folkestone, 39

Food, 9–10, 12, 85, 90, 102, 162, 186
Football, 82
France/French, 8–11, 13–15, 17, 21, 24, 26, 28, 34–6, 39–41, 45, 47, 55, 60–1, 63, 73, 79, 86–7, 93, 99–100, 103, 105, 107, 109–10, 112, 116, 119–20, 126, 134–6, 138–9, 141, 146, 153, 163, 166–7, 177, 183–186
French Army, 17, 21, 28, 41, 45–7, 63, 73, 101, 103, 110, 153
French, Field Marshal Sir John, 136, 138
Freedoms, 12

Garde Civile, 47
German Army, 17, 31, 40, 47–53, 58–9, 63–4, 70, 72–4, 77–8, 82–3, 93, 99, 100, 102, 105–106, 113, 125, 128, 148, 152, 166–8, 181–2
Germany/Germans, 9–14, 16, 23, 25–6, 36, 39–40, 62, 64, 105, 118, 122, 126–7, 129, 131–2, 148, 153, 156–7, 178, 181, 183–5
German Navy, 13, 29, 49–50, 62, 157, 166–7, 183, 186
Government, 11–14, 20, 38–9, 88, 96, 141, 166, 176, 183–4
Grand Roue de Paris, 15
Grey, Sir Edward, 136, 183
Guildhall, 83, 96, 169, 184–5

Hartlepool, 160, 186
Holland, 8, 83, 129, 183
Home Front, 7–8, 60, 107, 112, 157, 182
Horse Guards Parade, 42
Hospital(s), 13, 20, 87, 113–23, 155–6, 163, 165, 172–3, 184
Hospital ships, 155, 172
Hull, 156
Hungary, 34, 54, 57, 130, 183

India, 45, 70, 86–7, 133, 136, 171
Ireland/Irish, 8–9, 21, 139–41, 183

Japan, 8, 182, 184
Jellicoe, Admiral Sir John, 66, 139, 183

Kaiser Wilhelm II, 9–11, 20, 25, 37, 49, 89, 119, 129, 131, 183, 185
Kent, 7
King Albert, 138, 183
King Friedrich III, 130
King George V, 11, 17, 20, 68–70, 81, 87, 131, 135–6, 183–5
King Ludwig III, 91, 130
King Wilhelm II, 91, 129
Kitchener, 41, 69, 73, 137, 182–3, 185

Labour(ers), 13–14, 178, 184
Liverpool, 69
Liquor, 184
Lloyd George, David, 137, 184–5
London, 10–13, 20, 35, 43–4, 61, 68, 83, 86, 103–104, 115, 169, 175, 177, 182, 184–6
Lord Curzon, 169
Lord Fisher, 139, 185
Lord Haldane, 137
Lord Tredegar, 172–3
Lorraine, 36, 183
Ludendorff, 132

Manoeuvres, 17, 126
Manpower, 113
Meat(s), 88
Mehmed V, 130
Miners, 184
Mines/minelayer/sweeper, 106, 154, 156
Mobilisation, 10–11, 22–30, 37–8, 49–50, 61, 84, 92, 183

Müller, Capt, 133
Munitions, 13, 177–8

National Relief Fund, 183
Neutrality, 8, 41, 84, 183
Newcastle, 108
Norway, 183

Pankhurst, 183–4
Paris, 9, 11, 15, 24, 28, 34, 36, 45–6, 58–9, 95, 100, 103, 116, 141–2, 158, 163–5, 184, 186
Parliament, 183, 185
Patriotism, 42, 169
Peace, 9, 11, 13, 107, 139, 169, 183–4
Petrograd/St Petersburg, 99, 121
Plymouth, 115, 185
Poincaré, Raymond, 134
Police, 10–12, 38, 185
Post/Post Offices/Postage/Postal Orders, 10, 12, 82, 91, 180, 183
Postcards, 82, 84, 87, 108, 127, 151–2
Press, 13–14, 131, 183
Prices, 9–10, 13, 184
Prince Albert, 136
Prince Charles of Austria, 134
Prince Ernest August of Hannover, 131
Prince Heinrich XLVI, 125
Prince Louis of Battenburg, 138, 185
Prince Rupprecht of Bavaria, 133
Prince Wilhelm, 131
Prince of Wales, 16, 61, 68, 136, 183
Princess Mary, 68, 137
Princess Viktoria Luise, 131
Princip, Gavrilo, 185
Prisoners of War, 8, 105–106
Propaganda, 14, 59, 99, 102, 107, 167
Prussia, 14, 85, 100, 129, 143–6, 165, 183

Queen Alexandra, 68
Queen Charlotte, 118
Queen Mary, 68, 131, 184
Queen Victoria, 10

Raids, 157, 186
Railway(s), 12, 27, 51, 63–4, 183
Reading, 6, 39, 45, 64, 88, 93, 114, 125, 147, 171
Recruiting/recruitment, 11, 23, 43–5
Recruits, 7, 11, 42, 44, 71, 75–6, 185
Red Cross, 84, 89, 93, 112, 117–18, 124, 146, 163, 170–3, 181
Refugees, 8, 12, 85, 96, 141–4, 146, 148–9
Reichstag, 9, 11
Religion, 109, 111
Restaurants, 11
Reservists, 10, 18, 25, 27–30, 39, 46, 48, 50, 58, 128
Retail Food Price Index, 186
Riots, 95
Roberts, Field Marshal, 139–40, 185
Royal Naval Division, 66, 184
Royal Navy, 17, 30, 106–107, 126, 154, 157, 183
Russia, 8–10, 25, 85, 99–101, 104–105, 113, 121, 143, 145–6, 168, 183–4, 186

Sabotage, 64
Scarborough, 154, 161, 163, 186
Schools, 10, 13, 117, 185
Scotland, 12
Serbia, 9, 63, 183
Shell(s), 14, 161–3
Shortage(s), 9, 14, 43, 71–2, 78, 91, 102
Skilled workers, 178
Soup kitchens, 184
Southend, 186

Special Constables, 174, 184
Spies/spying, 8, 12, 63, 95–6, 183, 185–6
Spencer's Wood, 20
Stock Exchange, 9, 23
Suffragettes, 184
Sugar, 185
Sweden, 183
Switzerland, 62, 84, 183

Taxis, 10
Territorials, 11, 19, 47, 61, 65–7
Tirpitz, 132
Tower of London, 13, 185
Training, 7, 18, 43, 56, 58, 65–6, 72–5, 77–8,
    80–1, 90, 126
Troops, 10–11, 17–18, 21, 27, 32, 36–7, 45,
    55–8, 62, 65, 67, 69–70, 72–4, 82–3, 86–8,
    97, 101, 108–10, 139, 150, 167–8, 170, 180,
    185
Turkey/Ottoman Empire, 130, 185
Turkish Army, 55

U-boats, 154
Unemployment, 184
Unions, 183

VAD, 13, 174

Vienna, 28, 32–3, 54, 57, 59, 101, 143
Viviani, René, 134, 183
Volunteers, 13, 30, 40–1, 53, 62, 70–1, 73, 78,
    82, 93, 117–18, 142, 163, 175–6, 184
von Falkenhayn, 133
von Müller, 133
von Spee, 132

Wages, 12
Wales/Welsh, 108
War Loan 185
Weddigen, Kapitänleutnant, 134
Wellington Barracks, 107
Wellington Club, 114
Wellington College, 20, 21, 125
Whitby, 155, 186
White City, 75, 78
Whitehall, 42
Women, 11, 13–14, 20, 40, 43, 45, 62, 89, 91,
    93, 159, 163, 168, 173, 176–7, 183–5
Wounded, 13, 36–7, 87, 91, 94, 111–16, 119,
    121, 124, 150, 159, 184

Zanzibar, 185
Zeebrugge, 186
Zeppelin, 7, 14, 86, 157